Advance Words for

INTEGRATED LIVES

"Dale Stoll has captured a key for God's people in this important work. His words bring the kind of insights that are all too rare in the church today: In a world of promises unfulfilled, God still delivers. His call for us to get real and do the same is needed. This book will give you a deeper understanding of the kingdom of God—the central focus of Jesus. I'm sure it will make a difference."

- **Dr. David Cannistraci,** Senior Pastor of Gate Way City Church, San Jose, CA, and author of *Apostles and the Emerging Apostolic Movement* and *God's Vision for Your Church.*

"Many thoughtful Christians have an uneasy feeling. We know that something is fundamentally wrong with the 21st century church. We see the superficial Christian faith in our churches and ministries but it's hard for us to pinpoint what the root causes are. Perhaps in response we preach harder and pray more but underneath the root problems elude us. In a refreshing and clear way, Dale Stoll takes us back to the core issues. What is the good news of God's kingdom? What are its claims? What is to be our response? Thanks, Dale, for blowing away our confusion and pointing us anew to Christ and his kingdom!"

- **Jim Egli,** Ph.D., Lead Small Group Pastor of The Vineyard Church, Urbana, IL and author of *Upward, Inward, Outward, Forward* and *Encounter God.*

"*Integrated Lives* comes from the pen of a practitioner, not just a theoretician. Dale Stoll has nurtured local community and has contributed to the Body of Christ at large. This presentation of good news is a fresh, bold new look at today's generation in the light of the Gospel. This book is a challenge and a call to finally make the transition from worldly culture to Kingdom culture, from fragmented gospels to the integrating gospel of the kingdom proclaimed by Jesus and the early Church. Through these pages, our view of the world and our understanding of our place in it will change. Be ready to become a greater influencer and affect the world for Christ."

- **Sergio Scataglini**, former Senior Pastor of Puerta del Cielo in Argentina and founder of Scataglini Ministries, Inc., author of *The Fire of His Holiness* and *The Twelve Transgressions.*

"Dale Stoll, with teaching that is clear and firm, unfolds the Good News of God for our contemporary world. The Gospel of the Kingdom is linked here with a key to engaging postmodern culture—authenticity. Dale's challenge to the church in these pages is to lay aside "fragmented" versions of the gospel and embrace an integrating one that transforms individuals and societies."

- **Keith Yoder**, Ed. D., Founder of Teaching The Word Ministries, Leola, PA and author of *Healthy Leaders.*

INTEGRATED LIVES

Living the Good News of Jesus

DALE L. STOLL

RESTORATION PRESS, BRISTOL, IN 

Cover Design: Harriet Miller

ISBN 978-0-9773643-3-6

Library of Congress Control Number: 2009906313

CONTENTS

CONTENTS

ACKNOWLEDGMENTS

Very little, if anything, of significance is accomplished alone in God's kingdom. We each are part of Christ's new community, the Church, and the gifts and abilities of one add to those of another to accomplish the work God assigns to us. So it has been with this book.

Many people have impacted my life for the better and have contributed to this book in one way or another! It would be impossible to recognize them all. However, some stand out in the crowd.

First, there is Gwen, my wonderful wife of 40 years. Without the unselfish giving of herself to care for our children and her faithful, never-ending support, I would not have attempted this project. I have no adequate words to describe what she means to me.

Then there are Harold Bauman and Keith Yoder, my overseers, mentors, and friends. These two brothers have encouraged, supported, challenged, and corrected me when needed—and I am a better person for it. I long for every minister to experience the kind of oversight and loving accountability they have extended to me over many years.

I also am very grateful for the support and encouragement expressed by all the sisters and brothers who partner with me in Radical Restoration Ministries. They have read my writings and offered helpful suggestions that have always stimulated my thinking. Their feedback on this manuscript contributed to a final product that will be more helpful to its readers.

Finally, two people who worked directly with me on this book have greatly enhanced the end result. Harriet Miller has been responsible for the cover design, artwork, layout and production. My editor, Ruth Ford, has made countless improvements to my writing. I am very grateful for their invaluable assistance.

May God be glorified, and may the work of the kingdom go forth as together we serve Jesus, our Lord and Savior and soon-coming King!

WHERE I STAND

All of us have a place where we stand. This place has been shaped by our life experiences—the books we've read, places we have been, people we have conversed with, movies we have watched, etc. The Apostle Paul understood that where we stand affects our ability to see things clearly:

> For now we see only a reflection as in a mirror; then we shall see face to face. Now I know in part; then I shall know fully, even as I am fully known. (1 Cor. 13:12)

We are still in the "now." We see only a reflection and we know only in part. That should not cause us to despair, but should keep us humble.

My first Bible came to me as a Christmas gift from my parents when I was 13 years old. It was a King James Version, and had a reading schedule in the front that, if followed, would take one through the Bible in a year. I don't know how many times I started that schedule, only to give up somewhere in Leviticus. I just got lost in all the details of Israelite law in the Shakespearian English of the King James Version.

Several years later I read my first modern language version of the Bible, and I have been reading it ever since. I have now been all the way through it too many times to count. It has truly proven to be "a lamp to my feet and a light for my path" (Ps. 119:105).

I have come to understand the Bible as the reliable record of God's self-revelation in human history. It has greatly shaped where I stand. I have also come to understand that life is found in a person, not in a book. Jesus chided his Jewish contemporaries with these words:

> You study the Scriptures diligently because you think that in them you possess eternal life. These are the very Scriptures that testify about me, yet you refuse to come to me to have life. (John 5:39,40)

In this book, I hope to introduce you to a person, the Jesus revealed in the Scriptures as promising life—the integrated life. There are other versions of Jesus around today, even as there were in Paul's day. He wrote about those who preach "a Jesus other than the Jesus we preached" (2 Cor. 11:4). The problem with these "other Jesuses," whether in the first century or the 21st, is that they fail to bring life—the integrated life.

To introduce you to the real Jesus, I will often refer to Scripture—that reliable record of God's self-revelation that culminated in the person of Jesus. I trust my words will whet your appetite to read more of those ancient words for yourself. To help you make the connection between my words and Scripture, a list of abbreviations used in this book is found on the following page.

May God bless you and reveal himself to you as you read. And may that revelation shape the place where you stand as it has shaped mine!

Dale Stoll
July, 2009

ABBREVIATIONS

The Old Testament
(Listed Alphabetically)

Abbreviation	Book
Amos	Amos
1 Chron.	1 Chronicles
2 Chron.	2 Chronicles
Dan.	Daniel
Deut.	Deuteronomy
Eccles.	Ecclesiastes
Esther	Esther
Exod.	Exodus
Ezek.	Ezekiel
Ezra	Ezra
Gen.	Genesis
Hab.	Habakkuk
Hag.	Haggai
Hosea	Hosea
Isa.	Isaiah
Jer.	Jeremiah
Job	Job
Joel	Joel
Jon.	Jonah
Josh.	Joshua
Judg.	Judges
1 Kings	1 Kings
2 Kings	2 Kings
Lam.	Lamentations
Lev.	Leviticus
Mal.	Malachi
Mic.	Micah
Nah.	Nahum
Neh.	Nehemiah
Num.	Numbers
Obad.	Obadiah
Prov.	Proverbs
Ps.	Psalms
Ruth	Ruth
1 Sam.	1 Samuel
2 Sam.	2 Samuel
Song of Sol.	Song of Solomon
Zech.	Zechariah
Zeph.	Zephaniah

The New Testament
(Listed Alphabetically)

Abbreviation	Book
Acts	Acts
Col.	Colossians
1 Cor.	1 Corinthians
2 Cor.	2 Corinthians
Eph.	Ephesians
Gal.	Galatians
Heb.	Hebrews
James	James
John	John (Gospel)
1 John	1 John (Letter)
2 John	2 John (Letter)
3 John	3 John (Letter)
Jude	Jude
Luke	Luke
Mark	Mark
Matt.	Matthew
1 Pet.	1 Peter
2 Pet.	2 Peter
Philem.	Philemon
Phil.	Philippians
Rev.	Revelation
Rom.	Romans
1 Thess.	1 Thessalonians
2 Thess.	2 Thessalonians
1 Tim.	1 Timothy
2 Tim.	2 Timothy
Titus	Titus

INTRODUCTION

We, who come last, desire to see the first things and wish to return to them insofar as God enables us. We are like people who have come to a house that has been burnt down and try to find the original foundations. This is more difficult in that the ruins are grown over with all sorts of growths, and many think that these growths are the foundation, and say, 'This is the foundation' and 'This is the way in which all must go,' and others repeat it after them. So that in the novelties that have grown up they think to have found the foundation, whereas they have found something quite different from, and contrary to, the true foundation.

Peter Cheltschizki, Bohemia, 1440[1]

I have many memories of listening to my Dad tell stories. Some he told directly to me, but most I heard by eavesdropping as he told them to other adults.

One of my favorites was of a city-dweller going for a drive in the country and getting lost. Unable to find his way back to town, he stopped and asked a farmer who was working in his field: "Hey, I'm lost! How do I get back to town?"

The farmer scratched his head and drawled, "Well, I think I would go to the first crossroads and turn left....No, I think I would go to the second crossroads and turn left...Well, actually, if I wanted to go to town, I don't think I would start from here!"

That's a classic case of being honest, but not helpful. We all know that, concerning our life journey, our only starting point at any time is *where we are*. And if we are in denial of where we are, we will spend more time wandering around the countryside.

My starting point in pastoral ministry was at Tri Lakes Community Church, July 22, 1979. It has been quite a journey since then. I was quite successful, in some ways. The church grew from about 25 to over 275 in worship attendance. We completed a building program as we "enlarged the place of our tent" (Isa. 54:2)—the slogan for our building campaign. And, I survived as pastor for over 22 years in the same place! Now that's surely success! Or is it? How *do* we measure success in the church? That question has stayed with me over the years.

In the fall of 1985, I first read a report by George Gallup, Jr. reflecting the results of polling on religious issues over a 50-year period. Part of that report read as follows:

> Certain basic themes emerge from the mass of survey data collected over the period of five decades—themes that probably apply not only to the 50-year history of scientific polling, but to the history of the nation:
>
> - The widespread appeal or popularity of religion
> - The gap between belief and commitment; between high religiosity and low ethics
> - The glaring lack of knowledge
> - What would appear to be a failure, in part, of organized religion to make a difference in society in terms of morality and ethics
> - The superficiality of faith[2]

Around that time, I read another report. I can no longer document it, but I'll never forget it. It stated, in essence, that concerning the behaviors of lying and cheating, there was little or no significant difference between churched and unchurched people. These two reports became a new starting point for me, beginning a quest that has continued to this day: *Why* do we see this "gap between belief and commitment"?

Throughout the years since then, Gallup, George Barna, and others have consistently reported this huge gap between belief and behavior within the church. In Gallup's words:

> When our nation's four to five hundred thousand clergy address their congregations each week, they face people whose choices contradict their values...(they) preach to boomers who believe in angels but cheat on taxes, college students who pray but regularly get drunk.[3]

I didn't have to read the surveys to see this discrepancy: I saw it in many of the people I loved and served—and too often in my own life.

As I grappled with these observations and questions over the last 20 years, I arrived at two conclusions. First, the only reliable measure of success for the church must be transformed and integrated lives. Church growth won't cut it. The number and quality of programs don't tell us what we need to know. Average church attendance doesn't. The number of small groups doesn't. The number of baptisms doesn't give a definitive answer. These may all be indicators to one degree or another, but only transformed and integrated lives truly tell the story—because only God can change a life. We can produce just about every other statistic on our own—if we are gifted and smart enough—but we can't transform a life to look like Jesus.

What is an integrated life? To integrate is "to form into a more complete, harmonious, or coordinated entity often by the addition or arrangement of parts or elements."[4] An integrated life is one in which all the parts fit together as a whole. Sometimes the parts need to be arranged differently; sometimes something is missing that must be added. An integrated life is a life of integrity—where what we believe, what we say, and what we do all line up and fit together. It is a life that looks more and more like Jesus as time passes.

The opposite of an integrated life is a fragmented one—one where it often seems no matter how hard you try, you just can't get it all to fit together. It is a very common problem in our world today—and in the contemporary church—for reasons that will become evident in the pages of this book.

Now if transformed and integrated lives are the measure of success, Gallup's poll results must cause us to question how successful we have been. I concluded that my 22 years were not that successful. It certainly was not all bad—some good things were happening—but not many lives were being transformed and integrated into a life-giving whole.

In October 2001 I resigned my pastorate, another new starting point. I wanted to give my full time to the pursuit of understanding why we are where we are, and to helping other younger pastors go beyond where I was able to go. The years since then have brought me to my second conclusion: Problems at the most foundational level have produced these results.

Dallas Willard raises a very good question: "Should we not at least consider the possibility that this poor result is not *in spite of* what we teach and how we teach, but precisely *because of it*?[5] (emphasis added). Remember, if we live in denial we will remain lost in the countryside!

Just as Peter Cheltschizki wrote over 500 years ago, today's church has "novelties" that have grown over and obscured the true foundation, and now are believed to *be* the foundation. Yet, they are actually "quite different from, and contrary to, the true foundation." These "novelties" today go as deep as the very message we have proclaimed as the gospel. In our efforts to simplify the gospel and to make it "relevant" to our culture, we have ended up with several versions of the good news that are no longer that good—they lack the power to transform and integrate life. They are fragmented gospels—and they produce fragmented lives. Again, Gallup expresses it well:

> Contemporary spirituality can resemble a grab bag of random experiences that does little more than promise to make our eyes mist up or our heart warm. We need perspective to separate the junk food from the wholesome, the faddish from the truly transforming.[6]

It's not that these fragmented gospels contain no truth; it's just that we have taken portions of God's truth and mixed them with spiritual "junk food." In the process, we have changed the overall message—and the effectiveness of that message.

How do we understand our challenging time? What fragmented gospels are around today, and why do they fail to integrate our lives? What *is* the "good news of the kingdom" that Jesus proclaimed? How do we take hold of it—and follow him in life from that point forward? How do we share this good news with others in a respectful and effective way? These are some of the questions we will answer in these pages.

Perhaps you have embraced a fragmented gospel, and consequently you've seen little real change. Perhaps you long for something different, but you feel stuck. Then this book will help you discover the authentic "good news of the kingdom of God and the name of Jesus Christ" (Acts 8:12) proclaimed in the New Testament. You will find that God is more than able to get you unstuck and to integrate your life into a beautiful whole.

Maybe you have been a long-time follower of Jesus, but you still have a hard time explaining God's kingdom to someone else. Maybe you have never tried to do so. If that's the case, this book will encourage you and build your faith that you can! After all, if we are following Jesus, can we ignore the one subject that Jesus talked about more than any other?

Finally, this book will prove to be a helpful tool to pass on to—and discuss with—your seeker friends. Most people who decide to trust Jesus with their lives are led there by friends who care enough to invest in their lives. Sharing this book with your friends will introduce Jesus and his message to them—and give them the possibility of a new starting point in their life journey!

My prayer for you is the same as Paul wrote to Jesus' followers in Rome in the first century:

> So here's what I want you to do, God helping you: Take your everyday, ordinary life—your sleeping, eating, going-to-work, and walking-around life—and place it before God as an offering. Embracing what God does for you is the best

> thing you can do for him. Don't become so well-adjusted to your culture that you fit into it without even thinking. Instead, fix your attention on God. You'll be changed from the inside out. Readily recognize what he wants from you, and quickly respond to it. Unlike the culture around you, always dragging you down to its level of immaturity, God brings the best out of you, develops well-formed maturity in you. (Rom. 12:1,2, *THE MESSAGE*)

May you think before you just fit in. May you fix your attention on God and be changed from the inside out. May you and those you care about experience integrated lives together, as you join me in this journey. May this be a new starting point for you!

1

FRACTURED, FRAGMENTED AND FRAZZLED!

The thief comes only to steal and kill and destroy;
I have come that they may have life, and have it to the full.

Jesus, John 10:10

He (Jesus) is before all things, and in him
all things hold together.

Paul, Colossians 1:17

"Would you describe your life as more fragmented or more integrated? Does it fit together and feel like a whole—or does it seem more like a lot of disconnected pieces?"

It was a Thursday evening in the fall of 1999. I was addressing the leadership community of the church I had served as Senior Pastor for twenty years. I'm not sure why I asked that question. Maybe I was feeling fragmented myself. Maybe I was still in a reflective mood from my sabbatical that had ended a couple of months earlier. I had spent four months resting from the rigors of everyday ministry and reflecting on what I had learned from my years of pastoral ministry.

Whatever my reason for asking, I was surprised at what I heard in response. Overwhelmingly, the reply was "more fragmented than integrated." I heard things like:

- "Work takes almost all of my time."
- "My family is going in too many directions."
- "Church requires a lot of my attention."
- "I have to run like crazy to keep up with the finances."
- "There just isn't enough time to get everything done."

These were not people hanging around the fringes of the church—these were the twenty-some persons at the core of our congregation.

I left that meeting with a host of questions. Why do we feel this way? Do we not know how to set priorities? Is this just a problem of our little group, or is it more widespread? What about our culture as a whole? Are things getting more integrated or more fragmented? What's happening to our world? This book grew from those questions.

Great Expectations

I graduated from high school in 1966, a time of great expectations. We were in the middle of the race to the moon. The Soviet Union launched Sputnik 1 in October 1957, and the United States answered with Explorer 1 in January 1958. President Kennedy promised in 1961 that we would put a man on the moon before the end of the decade, and we would beat the Russians in the process. That goal was realized when Neil Armstrong first stepped on the moon on July 20, 1969—which also happened to be my wedding day!

Another exciting development—perhaps of equal importance but less publicized—occurred at the same time. The ARPAnet, forerunner of the Internet, went live in 1969. The first e-mail was sent in late 1971 between two mainframe computers sitting in the same room, initiating an entirely new era in communications.

The wonder of scientific and technological breakthroughs implied that life could only get better. Both the music and the writing of the time predicted that we were on the verge of a new era of peace and harmony. It was the dawning of a new age, "The Age of Aquarius." A popular song by that title promised a time of "harmony and understanding, sympathy and trust abounding" just around the corner![1]

In 1970, Charles A. Reich expressed the same theme of a new age of harmony, wholeness and beauty in his book *The Greening of America*:

> There is a revolution coming. It will not be like revolutions of the past. It will originate with the individual and with culture, and it will change the political structure only as its final act. It will not require violence to succeed, and it cannot be successfully resisted by violence. It is now spreading with amazing rapidity, and already our laws, institutions and social structure are changing in consequence. It promises a higher reason, a more human community, and a new and liberated individual. Its ultimate creation will be a new and enduring wholeness and beauty—a renewed relationship of man to himself, to other men, to society, to nature, and to the land. This is the revolution of the new generation … .[2]

Aquarius went to number one on Billboard for six straight weeks and remained in the Top 40 for 16 weeks, and *The Greening of America* was required reading on many college campuses in the early '70s. But what has happened since then? Have we experienced this promised new era of peace and harmony? Are things more integrated and whole? Or, are things more fragmented than ever? Has life greened up or browned out? Let's look at a few statistics and some experiential evidence to help answer those questions.

- By 1991, the US crime rate per 100,000 inhabitants was 313% of the 1960 rate. Although the rate has moderated some since then, it remains considerably higher than it was in 1960.[3]
- The divorce rate increased 42% from 1970 to 1985. It has been decreasing since then, but not because couples are getting along better! Rather, more couples are living together without getting married. Approximately 50% of all first marriages now end in divorce, and by 2002, 31% of all children lived in single parent homes.[4]
- While the US population increased 45% from 1980 to 2005, the number of consumer bankruptcies increased by 567%.[5] In a

recent survey, finances were the most important stress factor for the three-fourths of Americans who said they frequently feel stress in their daily lives.[6]

- Each day in 2002 in the United States, about 2,450 children were found abused or neglected, and each day an average of four of these children died. As a foster parent of 22 children and adoptive parent of three, I identify with these figures. While I do not have statistics from earlier years, I've witnessed an alarming trend. Child abuse and neglect are growing problems.[7] To illustrate this point: Recently, the stepmother of a four-year-old girl in my home state taped the little girl's wrists together and her mouth shut and then proceeded to beat her to death with a broken cutting board while the girl's father stood by. This was not an isolated incident of uncontrollable rage—when sheriff's deputies responded to the 911 call, discovering the child's battered and lifeless body, it was their 44th visit to the home over a five-year period.[8]

- While plagues and pandemics have been greatly reduced, the occurrence and cost of lifestyle illnesses are soaring. Despite research indicating the relationship between certain behaviors and illnesses, we keep making the same lifestyle choices. A recent study showed the seven most common chronic health conditions—cancer, hypertension, heart disease, pulmonary conditions, diabetes, stroke, and mental illness—cost more than one trillion dollars each year in terms of treatment and lost productivity. These diseases often connect to lifestyle choices such as smoking, alcohol and drug abuse, overeating, overwork, stress, lack of sleep, etc. This same study found that, if these problems remain unaddressed, the number of cases diagnosed in those seven illness categories will increase 42% by 2023, for a total economic impact of $4.2 trillion.[9]

- Around the world, ethnic and religious wars are increasing in number and intensity. The events of September 11, 2001 removed any remaining illusions of peace and harmony being just around the corner. And, one outcome of the ensuing "War on Terror" seems to be more "terrorists."

- Each election year reveals that we seem more polarized and angrier than ever before. Actually, we don't need to wait for an election year to reveal this: Who hasn't encountered road rage?

- Finally, just after writing the above paragraph, I watched a news video on the internet about five people stepping over the body of a woman who lay dying in a convenience store after being stabbed. One person even took a picture. No one helped, and the woman died.

So much for "harmony and understanding, sympathy and trust abounding." Obviously, the fragmentation experienced by our leadership community was not peculiar to us. It's a widespread phenomenon in our time. But why are we so fractured, fragmented and frazzled? I see several reasons, beginning with the simple fact that we live in a very confusing and disorienting time. We are experiencing significant change on several fronts. In fact, we may be facing more changes than any other culture in recorded history.

LIVING IN A SEAM OF HISTORY

A seam is the place where two distinct things are joined together. Two pieces of fabric are united to make a garment. Two pieces of metal are welded to form one part of an instrument or machine. A seam in history is similar. It is the time when two distinct eras or periods meet, when one time is drawing to a close and another is beginning.

A seam joining two pieces of fabric or metal can be either narrow or wide, depending on how much the two pieces overlap. So it is with seams in history. For those of us who live in the United States, September 11, 2001 is an example of a very narrow seam in history. What began as a normal Tuesday morning suddenly changed when hijacked airplanes flew into the twin towers of the World Trade Center, into the side of the Pentagon in Washington, and into the ground in Pennsylvania. In one day, a time of peace became a time of war. A time of security became a time of anxiety for many.

Most seams in history are much wider, as two eras overlap for an extended period. In some cases, several decades or even a century can pass, from the leading edge of change to the time of substantial replacement by a new era.

This present period is a historical seam on at least three major fronts—economics, culture, and worldview.

An Economic Seam

From earliest recorded history until the 18th century, agriculture drove the world's economies. Concentrated effort produced sufficient food for the population.

In the 18th century, two things produced great change. First, agricultural improvements, such as crop rotation for higher yields and scientific animal breeding for higher quality and quantity of meat, facilitated adequate food production. Second, applying power-driven machinery to manufacturing ushered in the Industrial Revolution.

People were living in a historical seam that produced great upheavals of social change. Since less labor was needed on the farm, many moved to cities to work in factories. Charles Dickens' classic *A Tale of Two Cities* was set in France and England in 1775, in this time when an agricultural society became an industrial one. The book opens with these famous lines:

> It was the best of times, it was the worst of times, it was the age of wisdom, it was the age of foolishness, it was the epoch of belief, it was the epoch of incredulity, it was the season of Light, it was the season of Darkness, it was the spring of hope, it was the winter of despair.

This was literally true of the time, as England was experiencing spiritual revival and France bloody revolution. But the description could apply to most seams in history, as the challenges of change mingle with new opportunities.

The invention of the first freely programmable computer in 1936, and its first commercial application in 1951, ushered in another great time of economic change. It was the leading edge of the information society. The pace of change picked up with the first personal computer in 1981, and took a quantum leap forward with the Internet. While the Internet first went live in October 1969, it really took off in 1992, when commercial firms began offering Internet access to the general public. Anyone with a personal computer and a phone line now had access to information that, for centuries, had belonged only to the privileged few.

Availability fueled an explosion of information. At the end of 1992, only fifty web pages existed in the world. By the end of 2000, there were thirty million. In early 2007, estimates put the number at just under thirty *billion*![10] Broadband has supplanted dial-up access, so all this information is not only available, but it is available *fast!* And I can get it *on the go* with a device small enough to fit in my pocket!

Thus we are now living in another economic seam in history, one between an industrial society and an information society. Once again, great lifestyle changes are underway. The way people work, play and communicate has changed more in our lifetimes than in all prior history. All this change can disorient, contributing to the fragmentation we feel. It also contributes to the uncertainty in the world's economy.

A Cultural Seam

A second seam characterizing our time is the cultural seam between modernism and postmodernism. Humankind has only faced a cultural seam of this magnitude a few times in history, with the most recent being almost 500 years ago with the advent of the Enlightenment. Modern culture, dominated by reason and science, began to replace medieval culture that for a thousand years had been dominated by Christendom. Modern culture now is giving way to postmodernism. Both have contributed to the fragmentation of our lives.

Modernism and Compartmentalized Living

Throughout the modern cultural era—from about 1500 AD through the middle of the 20th century—many people looked to science and the material world to bring meaning and purpose to life. Science would answer every question and solve every problem, and material things would bring happiness, meaning and purpose.

Truly, we all have benefited from the rise of the scientific method. For example, who has not benefited from the advances of medical science? And what about technology? How different our lives would be without computers! Without refrigerators! Without microwave ovens! And how would we even survive without our cell phones?

But we must also understand the difference between scientific method and scientism. Scientific method is exactly that—a method for discovering. Scientism, on the other hand, is not a method, but a philosophy or religion. Scientism says human reason and science is *the* way to any and all truth. It operates in a closed system, with no place for God or anything supernatural. It also can be called naturalism.

The difference between scientific method and scientism is clearly illustrated in a debate carried in the November 5, 2006 issue of *Time Magazine*. The debate, entitled "God vs. Science," was between atheist evolutionary biologist Richard Dawkins and Christian geneticist Francis Collins.

TIME: Doesn't the very notion of miracles throw off science?

COLLINS: Not at all. If you are in the camp I am, one place where science and faith could touch each other is in the investigation of supposedly miraculous events.

DAWKINS: If ever there was a slamming of the door in the face of constructive investigation, it is the word miracle. To a medieval peasant, a radio would have seemed like a miracle...Once you buy into the position of faith, then suddenly you find yourself losing all of your natural skepticism and your scientific—really scientific—credibility. I'm sorry to be so blunt.

COLLINS: Richard, I actually agree with the first part of what you said. But I would challenge the statement that my scientific instincts are any less rigorous than yours. The difference is that my presumption of the possibility of God and therefore the supernatural is not zero, and yours is.

Collins is a brilliant scientist who mapped the human genome; Dawkins is also a brilliant scientist, but one who has embraced the philosophy of scientism.

Postmodern writer Walter Truett Anderson has noted, "Science, for many people in the modern era, merely replaced religion as the source of absolute truth."[11] But what really happened is that one religion replaced another.

John Dewey, recognized as the father of modern American education, concluded his book *A Common Faith* in 1934 by declaring, in humanism "are all the elements of a religious faith that shall not be confined to sect, class or race. Such a faith has always been implicitly the common faith of mankind. *It remains to make it explicit and militant.*"[12] (Italics added) Dewey recognized humanism for what it is—a religion.

The religion Dewey called humanism could more aptly be called scientism, naturalism, materialism, selfism, or paganism. All of these would be accurate. But it can hardly be called humanism. Humanism is defined as devotion to human welfare, but as Ravi Zacharias notes, "The farther we move from God, the more we devalue man."[13]

I think we must acknowledge that Dewey and those who followed him have accomplished what they set out to do. Their religion has largely replaced Christianity as the religion of the university and the marketplace—supported by the tax dollars of millions of Christians! But it hasn't made the world a more humane place.

As an end result, this cultural religion has tended to either squeeze God—and especially Jesus—totally out of the picture, or confine him to a religious realm considered irrelevant to everyday life. You can take God to church on Sunday, but don't try to take him to school or work with you!

This compartmentalized living has contributed much to our fragmentation. How does life fit together when it is divided into two separate compartments—especially when those two compartments have two opposite and competing religions? Compartmentalized living is a major legacy of modernism.

Postmodernism and Deconstruction

Optimism reigned in the 1950s. World War II—the war to end all wars—was over! Soldiers came home, and families were reunited. All those factories that had been supplying weapons and machines of war could produce things that people wanted to buy. The greatest consumer push in history was underway, and everything about the future looked rosy—or did it?

About the same time, a lot of young people began to realize that, despite our prosperity, many questions pertaining to meaning and purpose remained unanswered. They reacted to the world and to their parents' ways, and the cultural upheaval of the 60s was born. This reaction to modernism, developing over the last half of the 20th century, is known as postmodernism.

As we are still relatively early in the postmodern era, both postmodernism and one of its most central terms, deconstruction, prove to be very slippery to define. Frenchman Jacques Derrida first used "deconstruction" in the field of literature in the late 1960s. In simple terms, it implies that in reading literature you don't concern yourself with the author's intended meaning, but with its meaning to you.

As one person expressed it, "Deconstruction is a theory that 'eats itself' because it suggests that texts have no inherent meaning in them due to the unstable and 'liquid' nature of meanings that words suggest."[14] Frankly, after many attempts to find a definition of deconstruction that I could understand, I gave up. If texts themselves have no inherent meaning, how do you define anything?

While not quite as elusive as deconstruction, postmodernism itself has been defined in many ways. However, postmodern philosopher Jean-François Lyotard gets to the heart of the matter with his statement, "Simplifying to the extreme, I define postmodern as incredulity *(disbelief)* towards metanarratives."[15] A metanarrative is a "big story" that provides a comprehensive explanation of historical experience or knowledge. We could say it is a coherent worldview by which we interpret all of life.

There is a general fear in postmodernism that anyone who claims to have a "big story" will eventually attempt to impose it on others and do away with other competing "big stories." These fears are not without some basis, for we find examples in the case of Christianity and the Crusades, Islamists and Jihad, and in the shoving of Christianity out of public life by modernism. But after deconstructing all the big stories into a lot of little ones, postmodernists are faced with a big problem—without an integrating big story, life itself tends to deconstruct into many fragments.

Because we live in the seam between modernism and postmodernism, we see two very different ways of thinking, of seeing the world, coexisting in our time. Two people can use the same words to communicate very different messages, hindering any meaningful dialog. Perhaps the best illustration is the subject of truth. To a modern person, truth is objective, concrete, something that can be identified in the lab. Many postmodernists run to the opposite extreme, seeing "truth" only as a socially-constructed reality, as subjective as the people and cultures from which they originate. To these folks, each culture or subculture has its own "truth," and none is more valid than the others.

Postmodernism has some weaknesses, but it also has brought some correction to the excesses of modernism. One of its greatest contributions to people of faith is the unmasking of the myth that modern science and reason are totally objective, especially when it comes to the study of humanity. While psychologist Carl Rogers likely would not have classified himself as postmodern, his statement in a 1969 interview is very postmodern:

> I think psychology, especially university psychology, is really living by an outmoded model of science … . I think they have never faced the problems created by the scientist being both the scientist and the material of his science. It's something that no other science has really had to face, because it's just been a little peripheral problem that the human factor does enter into the reading of the dial or the photograph or whatever, even in the "hardest" of the physical sciences. But where you are not only the subject but the object of the science as well, it creates a great many new problems. I believe we have not yet found what science might mean as applied to the human being.[16]

Centuries ago, the Apostle Paul understood that none of us are totally objective, as he wrote, "For now we see only a reflection as in a mirror; then we shall see face to face. Now I know in part; then I shall know fully, even as I am fully known" (1 Cor. 13:12). All of us are a product of our past to some degree. Our experience has shaped how we see things—even how we read the Scriptures.

While postmodernists cling to varying degrees of relativism, not all have ruled out the possibility of absolute truth. After all, thinking postmodernists know the statement, "There is no absolute truth," is self-contradictory. Well-known postmodern scholar Stanley Fish writes, "The only means to absolute certainty is through revelation, something I do not rule out but have not yet experienced."[17] That understanding of truth is actually much closer to the Christian understanding than is the modern idea that truth is self-evident through reason alone. Faith in Christ is not unreasonable; it just goes beyond reason to include revelation.

In the western world, particularly here in the United States, I believe we are very near the middle of this seam in history. Never have we been more evenly divided on more issues. We see two frustrated groups of people with very different views of the world, talking past each other rather than to each other. Anger is growing all around us. It is hard to keep a level head and hold life together in the midst of this.

A Worldview Seam

As significant as these economic and cultural changes are, we are in another seam of even more significance, one that actually lies under the cultural seam. It is the seam between two fundamentally different and irreconcilable worldviews.

What is a worldview? It is something everyone has whether they realize it or not. A worldview is a set of presuppositions or basic beliefs about the world in which we live. It answers four basic questions:

- Origin – Where have we come from?
- Identity – Who are we?
- Problem – What has gone wrong with our world?
- Solution – What is the remedy?

As important as all four of these questions are, the most important is the first. Once this question is answered, the other three flow from it.

Ultimately, I see only two basic worldviews, God-centered or human-centered. There are many variations, but every worldview begins at one place or the other. And, where we begin greatly impacts where we end up. Either there is a God who created this world, including the human race in his image, or the human race has created god in our own image. The question is not, "Which came first, the chicken or the egg?" The real question is, "Which came first, God or the human race?"

As far back as 1841, Ludwig Feuerbach recognized the significance of this question in his book with the audacious title *The Essence of Christianity*:

> If human nature is the highest nature to man, then practically also the highest and first law must be the love of man to man. *Homo homini Deus est.* (Man's God is Man):—this is the great practical principle:—this is the axis on which revolves the history of the world.[18]

While I believe Feuerbach's conclusion was wrong—and about as far from the "essence of Christianity" as possible—he was right about the significance of the question. The axis of history does revolve around the question of whether "man's god is man," or whether there truly is a "God who is there"—to borrow a Francis Schaeffer title.

Feuerbach's human-centered worldview has now been dominant in our western educational system for some time. As a result, even those who would claim a God-centered worldview have accepted many ideas that grow from a human-centered one—often without thinking. This in turn leads to behaviors that, in many instances, are practical expressions of a human-centered worldview. This causes great confusion among Christians, as we have accepted these ideas without thinking through the implications.

I believe one of the Christian Church's greatest problems is the double-mindedness that is rooted in these conflicting worldviews. On the one hand, we have been influenced by the God-centered Scriptures taught in our churches. On the other, we have been greatly impacted by ideas advanced by the predominant human-centered culture. This double-mindedness has certainly added to the fragmentation of our lives.

A PERPLEXING QUESTION

Outlining these changes helps define why our culture is so fragmented, but those of us who are Christians are left with a perplexing question. Consider the words of Jesus and Paul from the beginning of this chapter: Jesus said "The thief comes only to steal and kill and destroy; I have come that they may have life, and have it to the full." Surely "life to the full" means more than what we are experiencing. Eugene Peterson certainly thought so when he paraphrased this verse in *The Message* as "I came so they can have real and eternal life, more and better life than they ever dreamed of." In addition to these words of Jesus himself, Paul wrote of him "He is before all things, and in him all things hold together."

So here is our perplexing question: If Jesus is the one who holds all things together, and he promises to give his followers more and better life, then why are our lives often as fragmented as our non-Christian neighbors?

That's what has been on my mind since I first asked that question of our leadership community in 1999. And while I will not give one oversimplified and all-encompassing answer, I have reached one conclusion: While the word "gospel" means "good news," what we are proclaiming as the gospel is *not*, for the most part, what Jesus, Paul, and the other early Christians proclaimed—and it is not particularly good news!

People are proclaiming a variety of "gospels" today. Some accommodate modernism, allowing for the compartmentalization of life. Others are more postmodernist, eliminating any integrating "big story." Still others are good as far as they go, but are incomplete. Unfortunately, they are all fragmented, so they contribute to the fracturing of our lives.

In the next chapter we will look closely at these fragmented gospels. Then we will be ready to reclaim the integrating one brought to a broken and fragmented world by Jesus and the New Testament Church.

APPLICATION TO LIFE

1. When you think of all the changes in our time, what feelings are stirred within you?

2. Are you open to seriously and honestly looking at your own life, including its degree of integration or fragmentation? If so, how would you describe it? Is it more like a beautiful flower with all its components as petals, integrated around an identifiable center—or more like petals randomly scattered on the ground without a real center?

3. How well do you know Jesus? Have you taken the time to seriously look at his life and his message as preserved for us in the four Gospels of the New Testament? How would you describe your relationship to him at this moment?

2 FRAGMENTED GOSPELS, FRACTURED LIVES

I am astonished that you are so quickly deserting the one who called you by the grace of Christ and are turning to a different gospel—which is really no gospel at all.

Galatians 1:6-7

It is hardly a wonder that the country that gave the world instant tea and instant coffee should be the one to give it instant Christianity.

A.W. Tozer[1]

More than thirty years ago, I sat in an Ancient Greek Philosophy class at Purdue University, studying Plato and his student Aristotle. I was not expecting a "God-encounter," but I had one!

Like most people, Plato (428-347 BC) sensed there was more to life than just the material world around us. He suggested the existence of a perfect *world of forms.* He saw material objects as imperfect copies of real forms. For example, he thought a visible, tangible, physical table was an imperfect copy of the perfect *form* of a table, existing in the unseen world of forms.

Plato's student Aristotle eventually said, in effect, "Even if there is a world of forms, we have no way to know for sure—we can't bridge the gap. Therefore, it's not worth thinking about." He chose to ignore anything not material.

Sitting in that classroom, I realized that both Plato and Aristotle were partially right, yet both also were very wrong. As Plato surmised, there is another world—a spiritual world. As Aristotle thought, we cannot bridge the gap, so we cannot know for sure. For the first time in my life, I understood the importance of revelation—God had bridged the gap from the other side! Since then, I have seen the Bible differently. Instead of just a book full of religious ideas and practices, I see it as the record of God's self-revelation to the human race through human history.

This self-revelation culminates in the person of Jesus—the One who came "to bring unity to all things in heaven and on earth" (Eph. 1:10). In God's kingdom, life is an integrated whole. Heaven has come to earth, and life is becoming integrated and whole again. This is the distinguishing characteristic of the authentic good news of God's kingdom, which Jesus lived and proclaimed.

And herein is the problem that led me to write this book: Largely through the influence of modernism and its legacy of compartmentalized living, a number of fragmented versions of the gospel have developed over the last hundred years or more—and they are something less than "good news." They fail to bring about integrated and reconciled lives. These fragmented gospels produce fractured lives.

FRAGMENTED GOSPELS

A fragment is part of a whole. Fragmented gospels contain part of the whole gospel, but other parts are missing, making them incomplete. Most emphasize certain scriptures while ignoring others that are equally important. Consequently, they fail to integrate fragmented lives. They fail to unite the spiritual realm and the physical realm into an integrated whole. Some are skewed toward the spiritual realm, losing an appropriate connection to real, everyday physical existence. Others are biased toward the material world, failing to value God and the spiritual realm.

The apostle Paul used strong language when referring to those who present a different gospel. He wrote, "…even if we or an angel from heaven should preach a gospel other than the one we preached to you, let that person be under God's curse!" (Galatians

1:8). As we have already seen, the word *gospel* means *good news*. A "different gospel" is *no* gospel, because it is *not* good news—it neither transforms our lives now, nor does it guarantee our future. So let's look at several of the fragmented gospels prevalent in today's world.

The "Try Harder" Gospel

The *try harder* gospel emphasizes scripture passages such as "Do not let sin reign in your mortal body so that you obey its evil desires" (Rom. 6:12). But it ignores "For it is by grace you have been saved, through faith—and this is not from yourselves, it is the gift of God—not by works, so that no one can boast" (Eph. 2:8-9).

People who embrace this fragmented gospel know that self-control is important. They know that truth must be lived out. The problem is, they think they can and must do this on their own: "I can do it if I just try harder." In a survey by the Pew Research Center, an organization that researches trends that shape our world, 29 percent of Christians say they are saved by their good actions.[2] Ultimately, that is pride; we don't like to depend upon others, not even upon God.

This gospel is unbalanced toward the physical realm, teaching that everything depends upon us and our actions. It does not adequately portray how God bridged the gap and entered our world to empower us to obey him. Typically, people who embrace the *try harder* gospel find no peace. They spend their lives trying to be religious—to do enough to make God happy, so that when they die, God will let them into heaven. This gospel can also be called a *works* gospel, for it proclaims that our good works earn our place in heaven—and hopefully we've done enough.

The problem is, how much is enough? The reformer Martin Luther (1483-1546) faced this question daily, until he had a genuine encounter with God. As a monk, he spent his life trying to please God and save himself. He pursued such things as fasting, vigils, and self-inflicted pain. He went beyond the monastery rules, doing such things as holding a vigil in a freezing cold room with no blankets.

In 1510, he journeyed to Rome and walked up the steps of St. Peter's on his hands and knees, kissing each step and repeating the "Our Father" prayer. When he reached the top, he stood and said, "Who knows whether it is so?"

Then one day, while studying Romans 1:17, he had a life-changing encounter with God. In his own words:

> Night and day I pondered until I saw the connection between the justice of God and the statement that "the just shall live by his faith." Then I grasped that the justice of God is that righteousness by which through grace and sheer mercy God justifies us through faith. Thereupon I felt myself to be reborn and to have gone through open doors into paradise. The whole of Scripture took on a new meaning, and whereas before the "justice of God" had filled me with hate, now it became to me inexpressibly sweet in greater love. This passage of Paul became to me a gate to heaven.[3]

People who embrace the *try harder* gospel often become the most religious people around—and the most miserable. They need to encounter God and his truth in the same way that Martin Luther did, so they can find freedom and joy in a reintegrated life.

The "Just Believe" Gospel

Most roads have a ditch on either side. If the *try harder* gospel is the ditch on one side, then the *just believe* gospel is the ditch on the other—and according to the Pew survey mentioned earlier, about an equal number of Christians are in both ditches (30 percent).[4] This gospel lifts up "Believe in the Lord Jesus, and you will be saved" (Acts 16:31). It embraces Ephesians 2:8,9 mentioned above, but fails to go on to verse 10: "For we are God's handiwork, created in Christ Jesus to do good works, which God prepared in advance for us to do."

In this *just believe* gospel, actions don't matter—just beliefs. The gospel gets reduced to "Jesus died for your sins." All we need to do is believe that. As Dallas Willard has pointed out, this version often reduces people's understanding of the gospel to two events—the first when they pray the sinner's prayer, and the second when they die and go to heaven.[5] It is certainly true that Jesus died to provide forgiveness of our sins. And, it is indeed good news that we have a home in heaven when we leave this earthly life. However, this oversimplification of the gospel is lopsided: it does not address how the good news of Jesus connects to everyday living.

For people who buy into the *just believe* gospel, Christianity is about praying the sinner's prayer, perhaps experiencing a great worship encounter once a week—and then living just like their non-Christian neighbors the rest of the week. To them, discipleship is a nice idea if you have time for it in the great American lifestyle.

This *just believe gospel* produces the "instant Christianity" that A.W. Tozer metioned in the quote at the beginning of this chapter:

> Instant Christianity came in with the machine age. Men invented machines for two purposes. They wanted to get important work done more quickly and easily than they ever could do by hand, and they wanted to get the work over with so they could give their time to pursuits more to their liking, such as loafing or enjoying the pleasures of the world. Instant Christianity now serves the same purposes in religion. It disposes of the past, guarantees the future and sets the Christian free to follow the more refined lusts of the flesh in all good conscience and with a minimum of restraint.[6]

This kind of oversimplification can also be tragic, for it can give people a false sense of security, as evidenced by these words of Jesus:

> Not everyone who says to me, 'Lord, Lord,' will enter the kingdom of heaven, but only those who do the will of my Father who is in heaven. Many will say to me on that day,

> 'Lord, Lord, did we not prophesy in your name and in your name drive out demons and in your name perform many miracles?' Then I will tell them plainly, 'I never knew you. Away from me, you evildoers!' (Matt. 7:21-23).

The *just believe* gospel originated from Western confusion over the meaning of the word "believe." To a Hebrew, believing in someone meant having faith in them, entrusting your life to them, following them. In fact, the word normally translated as *believe* in the New Testament is also translated as *entrust* or *trust in* (see John 2:24; 14:1; Rom. 15:13; Heb. 2:13).

We see similar confusion related to the word *faith.* In the Hebrew language of the Old Testament, to *have faith* is to *be faithful.* An Old Testament concordance will reveal that the word *faith* appears very few times in English translations. Usually it is translated *faithful.* Even where it is translated as *faith*, the context indicates the meaning is to be *faithful.* Usually it is about *keeping faith* or *breaking faith*, meaning to be *faithful* or *unfaithful.*

Although the New Testament was written in Greek, the culture was largely Hebrew. But we come to this New Testament through our contemporary Western mindset, which was derived largely from the Greek culture. We think abstractly. So, believing in God means we believe intellectually that he exists, which doesn't require us to trust him and follow him. But the New Testament addresses this problem:

> What good is it, my brothers and sisters, if people claim to have faith but have no deeds? Can such faith save them? Suppose a brother or sister is without clothes and daily food. If one of you says to them, "Go in peace; keep warm and well fed," but does nothing about their physical needs, what good is it? In the same way, faith by itself, if it is not accompanied by action, is dead.
>
> But someone will say, "You have faith; I have deeds." Show me your faith without deeds, and I will show you

> my faith by what I do. You believe that there is one God. Good! Even the demons believe that—and shudder. (James 2:14-19)

The *just believe* gospel has developed into a current version of New Testament era Gnosticism. This word comes from the Greek word for knowledge, *gnosis*. Gnostics believed in a true God who preceded creation and who, at some point in time, split into a plurality of gods. This plurality then emanated into everything, including humanity. Now a "divine spark," or "inner man," exists in every human, awaiting an awakening produced neither by faith nor by works, but by the secret knowledge of all this. Salvation, then, is not from sin by way of atonement, as in Christianity. Instead, it is a rescue from ignorance through "knowledge."

Gnostics saw creation and Fall as the same. The god who created things (the Demiurge) was a flawed expression of the true god, and so the creation itself was flawed. They saw Yahweh, the God of Israel, as this flawed expression of God, and saw the moral law of the Old Testament in a very negative light. Therefore, they were actually encouraged to rebel against this moral law.

By contrast, they saw Jesus not as the Son of God (Yahweh), but as a good "Messenger of Light" coming forth from the good and true God who existed before creation. They accepted some of Jesus' teachings, but they saw no connection between Jesus and Yahweh, Israel's God—the One Jesus addressed as "Father."

Everything was based on their personal experience of the knowledge of the divine inner spark. Because they saw the moral code as a flawed expression of a flawed god, their conduct was guided totally by their inner experience rather than any objective set of instructions. They were free to live according to their inner experience, wherever that might take them.

For some, this led to an extreme self-denial and even physical harm, because they saw their bodies as an evil part of the flawed creation. Most Gnostics, though, saw themselves as free from any behavioral constraints, which resulted in much loose living.

The contemporary spread of this *just believe* gospel, this present-day Gnosticism, has been recognized both inside and outside the church. Inside, research from George Gallup Jr. and George Barna documents the disconnect between peoples' beliefs and behaviors. Outside, Harold Bloom writes in *The American Religion*:

> We think we are Christian, but we are not. The issue is not religion in America but rather what I call the American Religion. ... There are indeed millions of Christians in the United States, but most Americans who think that they are Christians truly are something else, intensely religious but devout in the American Religion, a faith that is old among us, and that comes in many guises and disguises.[7]
>
> Ancient Gnosticism was an elite religion, or quasi-religion; the oddity of our American Gnosis is that it is a mass phenomenon. There are tens of millions of Americans whose obsessive idea of spiritual freedom violates the normative basis of historical Christianity, though they are incapable of realizing how little they share of what once was considered Christian doctrine.[8]

This *just believe* gospel proposes that one's own subjective experience of spiritual knowledge is all that matters. This message offers no solution for everyday life in the real physical world, and so its proponents continue to wallow in the mess of a fragmented life and a disintegrating culture.

Unfortunately, those who embrace this *just believe* gospel often live a resulting lifestyle too similar to that described by Paul in 2 Tim. 3:1-5:

> But mark this: There will be terrible times in the last days. People will be lovers of themselves, lovers of money, boastful, proud, abusive, disobedient to their parents, ungrateful, unholy, without love, unforgiving, slanderous, without self-control, brutal, not lovers of

> the good, treacherous, rash, conceited, lovers of pleasure rather than lovers of God—having a form of godliness but denying its power … .

Tragically, many non-Christians see the inability of this gospel to transform peoples' lives, and they write off Christianity as having no practical value, or worse yet, as something actually harmful.

The Modern "Jesus Seminar" Gospel

In the first chapter we saw that modernism focuses on the idea that science and human reason will explain and solve anything. The classic example of a thoroughly modern "gospel" is that developed by The Jesus Seminar, a group of scholars brought together by Robert W. Funk in 1985. Originally a group of over 200, it eventually dwindled to 74 Fellows who met twice each year for six years to supposedly determine which of the sayings recorded in the gospels as originating with Jesus were really authentic.

After a brief presentation and discussion of a particular saying, each Fellow would vote by anonymously dropping a colored bead into a box. A red bead meant this saying was "surely from Jesus." A pink one meant "probably the words of Jesus." Gray meant this was "not likely the words of Jesus." Finally, a black bead meant "definitely not the words of Jesus."

The result of The Jesus Seminar's work was published in *The Five Gospels* in 1993, with the text printed in colors corresponding to the beads. John Dominic Crossan, co-chair of The Jesus Seminar, makes the following claim:

> *The Five Gospels* is a red-letter day for the ethics of scholarship, for the moral demand that scholars of the Bible state clearly, openly, and honestly what are their sources, their methods, and their results, and, above all, that they come to conclusion and consensus.[9]

But there are several problems with this claim of full disclosure and consensus. First, the beads were dropped anonymously, so no one was accountable for the choice. Does this fit with "clearly, openly, and honestly?"

Second, when the beads were counted, they received a numerical value allowing for the calculation of a weighted average. This process completely covered significant disagreement among the Fellows. For example, the votes on one saying were split 20 percent red, 30 percent pink, 30 percent gray, and 20 percent black. In *The Five Gospels,* it is printed in gray, indicating scholarly consensus that the saying was not likely Jesus' words. In reality, there was no "scholarly consensus," for half of the Fellows thought this saying was surely or likely the words of Jesus. This is very misleading to readers of *The Five Gospels.*

Then there is the participants' obvious bias. This group of scholars did not reflect a full theological spectrum. They were handpicked by Funk, virtually assuring his desired outcome. In fact, Funk dismissed at least one Fellow who complained about the issues presented here, calling them an "intellectual sham."[10]

Funk clearly spelled out his biases in his paper "The Coming Radical Reformation: Twenty-one Theses." Included among these were: There is no personal god, no miracles, Jesus is not divine, prayer is meaningless, and the idea of atonement is a ridiculous carry-over from a primitive era, to name a few.[11] These are not scientific, scholarly conclusions, but religious convictions. Given these assumptions, the result of The Jesus Seminar is not surprising.

Robert Funk actually had a clear agenda—to come up with a different gospel, as he stated at the very first meeting of the Seminar:

> What we need is a new fiction that takes as its starting point the central event in the Judeo-Christian drama and reconciles that middle with a new story that reaches beyond old beginnings and endings. In sum, we need a new narrative of Jesus, *a new gospel, if you will*, that places

> Jesus differently in the grand scheme, the epic story.[12] (emphasis added)

Funk died in 2005 and The Jesus Seminar has lost much of its popularity. But Funk's ideas are still being set forth by retired Episcopalian Bishop John Spong. Spong has reduced Funk's theses from twenty-one to twelve and published his own version.[13] Spong posted this paper on the web and invited debate. In April 2004, I emailed him the following:

> Greetings, Bishop Spong:
>
> I have read with interest your message posted on the web, "A Call for a New Reformation."
>
> I have a question concerning the twelve theses included there. In general, these are stated in the negative, i.e. what you do not believe. Would it be possible for you to put in more positive statements what you do believe, especially concerning the following: God, Jesus, the human race, sin, the Bible, the cross, the resurrection, life after death.
>
> Perhaps you have already written this in another publication. If so, please advise.

I never heard from him, so I guess he considered my request unworthy of a response.

Funk, Spong, and others like them are ready to completely redefine the gospel and Christianity according to their modern worldview. They believe this will "save" Christianity by making it relevant in today's world and getting people back into church. Judging from the CBS *60 Minutes* interview with Bishop Spong, which aired May 21, 2000, some people are responding. But if the church to which they are returning no longer resembles Biblical Christianity, can it actually help them integrate their lives? Being culturally relevant is *not* just embracing all the assumptions of a fractured and compartmentalized modern culture. It *is* caring enough to understand the culture and offering the good news that

Jesus and the early church proclaimed. That is the avenue that can reintegrate life for its adherents.

The Postmodern "Create Your Own" Gospel

The advent of postmodern culture has birthed another fragmented gospel. I call it the *create your own* gospel. Proponents suggest that, since everything is relative, and texts have no meaning in themselves, everyone is free to create his or her own gospel. One woman described her process this way: "Mine was a patchwork God, sewn together from bits of rag and ribbon, Eastern and Western, pagan and Hebrew, everything but the kitchen sink and Jesus thrown in."[14]

Given that ideas are as diverse as people, it is not surprising that a number of *create your own gospels* exist today. For instance, consider one that I call the *role reversal gospel*. This belief system grew from the human-centered culture that dominates the present day. Because we are conditioned to see ourselves as the center of the universe, we become the masters, and God becomes the servant. The simple reality, though, is that we are not equipped to play the role of God! As has been said many times over the years and again recently in a popular song, "God is God and we are not!" As a friend once told me, "Being God is a big job! If you try it, it will probably kill you!"

In my early years of pastoral ministry, I worked with a young man named Danny. He had attended our youth group before I came as pastor, but he dropped out at some point. Soon after I came, he started coming to church occasionally, and we developed a friendship that has continued to this day—but not without its rocky moments!

Danny battled for years with a cross-addiction to alcohol and other drugs. He continued to struggle even after he made his first commitment to Jesus as his Savior. As our friendship grew, I noticed a very clear pattern of behavior. When life seemed to be under control, and things were going well, I saw very little of him.

When he got back into alcohol and drugs, and things fell apart, he would be back.

One day, when I wasn't ready to go back around the same mountain again, I looked at Danny and said, "You know what, man? You think God is your errand boy. When things are good, you don't give him the time of day. When they aren't, you want to be able to snap your fingers, and he's supposed to jump and straighten out your life again. I want to tell you something: He isn't your errand boy; He is God!"

This upset Danny, and I didn't see him again for a few months. Then one day my phone rang:

"Hey, this is Dan. Do you remember what you told me?"

"I've told you a lot of things! What are you referring to?"

"About me thinking that God was my errand boy?"

"Yes, I remember that," I responded. "What about it?"

"Well, I've been thinking about that, and I have come to the conclusion that you were right. I have been treating God as though he were my errand boy!"

Danny had accepted the *role reversal* gospel. He did what he wanted, and it was God's job to make sure things worked the way Danny wanted them to work.

Danny found out the hard way the truth in these words of E. Stanley Jones:

> We are finding out how not to do things, how not to live. We are finding out that there are some ways that life will not approve, and some ways that life will approve. We must come to terms with the nature of reality. We cannot evade it, twist it to our ends, make it approve what cannot be approved. There is something "given"; we don't produce it, we don't build it up—it is there, built into the nature of things . . . . We must come to terms with the moral universe or get hurt. We do not break the laws of God written into the nature of things. We break ourselves on them. Those laws are color-blind, class-blind, religion-blind. Break

> them, and you'll get broken. If you leap from a tenth-story window, you will not break the law of gravitation, you will only illustrate it.[15]

We prayed together and Danny confessed his rebellion against God. Danny's encounter with the living God initiated a new season in his life. Not everything has been rosy since, but today he is drug- and alcohol-free and is living a fruitful Christian life as a citizen of God's kingdom.

Another *create your own* gospel is known as the *prosperity gospel*—the idea that God wants you to be rich. You want a new silver-colored Lexus? You need to believe that God wants to bless you and that "whatever you ask for in prayer, believe that you have received it, and it will be yours" (Mark 11:24). After all, this is the Word of God and God has to honor his word!

A few years back, I listened to a preacher whipping a crowd into an emotional frenzy with a prosperity message. Not once did I hear anything about God's claim on our lives, only about our claim on his gold! I went home greatly grieved. The man forgot the words of Paul about "people of corrupt mind, who have been robbed of the truth and who think that godliness is a means to financial gain" (1 Tim. 6:5). Paul had a different message:

> But godliness with contentment is great gain. For we brought nothing into the world, and we can take nothing out of it. But if we have food and clothing, we will be content with that. People who want to get rich fall into temptation and a trap and into many foolish and harmful desires that plunge people into ruin and destruction. For the love of money is a root of all kinds of evil. Some people, eager for money, have wandered from the faith and pierced themselves with many griefs.
>
> But you, man of God, flee from all this, and pursue righteousness, godliness, faith, love, endurance and gentleness. (1 Tim. 6:6-11).

It is true that God loves us and wants to bless us, and that he invites us to petition him for "our daily bread"—the things we need for the life he wants us to have. But the motive behind our asking makes all the difference: "You do not have, because you do not ask God. When you ask, you do not receive, because you ask with wrong motives, that you may spend what you get on your pleasures" (James 4:2,3).

Finally, another example of the *create your own* gospel is the *self-fulfillment gospel.* Everywhere we go we hear the words, "You can be whatever you want to be." Actually, this is not true. If it were, I would either have played NBA basketball or major league baseball! But those who know me are aware that I have very little athleticism in my entire body. No amount of practice will change that.

This idea is actually pagan rather than Christian, because *if you could be whatever you wanted to be, you would be God.* A pagan alliance in our area some time ago had a logo saying, "Our fate is ours to create." I often wonder why so many Christians repeat this same idea without considering what they actually are saying. I don't tell my children they can be whatever they want—I tell them they can be what God designed them to be, and they will be fulfilled in that.

This is another case where a truth is pushed too far, and it becomes false. Certainly, we must cooperate with God if we want to become all that he designed us to be. But it is false to believe that we can single-handedly create whatever future we desire.

Alan Wolfe, an outside observer of Christianity, has noted this kind of *create your own* redefinition of the gospel in his book *The Transformation of American Culture: How We Actually Live Our Faith:*

> H. Richard Niebuhr documented the many ways in which Christ could become a transformer of culture. But in the United States culture has transformed Christ, as well as all other religions found within these shores. In every aspect of the religious life, American faith has met American culture—and American culture has triumphed … .

> The message of this book is that religion in the United States is being transformed in radically new directions.[16]

FRACTURED LIVES

Unfortunately, all of these fragmented gospels—"different gospels" as Paul called them—have one thing in common: They lack the power to help people become whole. They leave people self-centered, self-focused, and fractured—as we saw in chapter one. Only a gospel of reconciliation and integration can transform and restore people by God's power.

The good news of Jesus is the solid rock upon which the Christian life is built. As Paul wrote, "No one can lay any foundation other than the one already laid, which is Jesus Christ" (1 Cor. 3:11). If our understanding and experience of the foundation is off, how can we build solid, integrated and whole lives upon it?

The answer is....we can't! If we are to live wholesome and integrated lives, we must go back and build on the person of Jesus and the good news he proclaimed. That is the purpose of this book.

But before we can understand the good news of Jesus, we must first set the context into which he came. That is the "big story" of the Bible—the story of God's kingdom that Jesus demonstrated and proclaimed as he walked this earth. Then, through his death and resurrection, he opened the door for us to follow him to experience it for ourselves.

No Fear!

Lest the postmoderns among us get nervous, let me assure you that you have nothing to fear from anyone who is truly following Jesus. Why? Because Jesus, the very one who said, "All authority in heaven and on earth has been given to me" (Matt. 28:18), never imposed that authority on others.

Jesus demonstrated the power and authority of God's kingdom with his miracles. He spoke the words of truth of the kingdom, including "I am the way and the truth and the life. No one comes to the Father except through me" (John 14:6). He invited us with the words "Come! Follow me!" (Matt. 4:19). But he never used his power and authority to impose either himself or his message on anyone. He recognized and respected the free will given to the human race, and he would not violate it. A true disciple of Jesus will follow his example.

Yes, the Crusades of the Middle Ages were led by "Christians." But those leading the Crusades were not following Jesus. A simple reading of the gospels will show that Jesus did not do such things when he walked upon this earth. Jesus was a loving servant. He "did not come to be served, but to serve, and to give his life as a ransom for many" (Matt. 20:28). And, since "Jesus Christ is the same yesterday and today and forever" (Heb. 13:8), he won't do that today either.

So, join me in the next chapter as we look at the "big story" of God's kingdom! Then, in the rest of the book, we will look specifically at the good news of this kingdom that Jesus lived and proclaimed, and at how we can connect with him and follow him in life. I am convinced this is the way to see wholeness and integration come to our fractured, fragmented and frazzled lives! After all, he is the one in whom "all things hold together!"

APPLICATION TO LIFE

1. I stated that I have come to see the Bible as God's self-revelation to the human race through human history. How do you see the Bible? How would you explain the importance of revelation?

2. Have you encountered any of these fractured gospels? If so, what do you think of them? Do you agree with this chapter's premise that fractured gospels produce fragmented lives? Why or why not?

3. Which of these fractured gospels do you think are the most widespread in the church and in the world today?

3

THE BIG STORY OF THE KINGDOM

Jesus went through all the towns and villages, teaching in their synagogues, proclaiming the good news of the kingdom and healing every disease and sickness.

Matthew 9:35

A number of years ago, two women who had just visited our church for the first time stopped by my office. They both had been Jehovah's Witnesses, and through their own Bible study, they had left the Witnesses and had become Christians. "We have been in bondage once, and we don't want to be again. So we want to know what you believe," they explained.

I began talking about the kingdom of God. They were very surprised, and said, "Not many Christians talk about the kingdom of God. That's how we were trained to witness to nominal Christians. We would point out everything in the Gospels that Jesus said about the kingdom of God, and then ask them, 'Do they talk about that at your church?'"

Usually people answered, "Not really." They would ask, "Does that surprise you, given how much Jesus talked about it?" They told me, "Often we had them hooked at that point."

I was not surprised by their comments. As I traveled and spoke in churches throughout North America, I often asked Christians to "tell me about the kingdom of God." Most of the time, the response was a blank look! This is actually quite incredible, because in his three years of public ministry, Jesus talked more about this subject than any other.

In fact, once when people tried to keep him from leaving their area because they liked what he did and said, he responded, "I must proclaim the good news of the kingdom of God to the other towns also, *because that is why I was sent*" (Luke 4:43, emphasis added). This tells us that God's kingdom was central to Jesus—to his life, his ministry, and his message.

In our contemporary time, though, we face a couple of significant problems in understanding what he meant. First, we don't really use or understand the word "kingdom." If we hear it at all, it is likely in the context of the United Kingdom or its royal family. But the Queen and her family in the UK today have much to do with tradition and pomp, but little to do with real authority and governance. That is handled by the democratically-elected Parliament and the Prime Minister. Because that's our experience, we are likely to understand Jesus' words in the same way, with "the kingdom of God" meaning little more than religious pomp and ceremony.

Second, when we do encounter one or more of the few remaining kingdoms, they tend to operate the way kingdoms have always operated in our world—maintaining control through the threat or use of force. Yet, Jesus said his kingdom was very different from that. Once when addressing his followers, called "disciples" in the New Testament, he said:

> "You know that the rulers of the Gentiles lord it over them, and their high officials exercise authority over them. Not so with you. Instead, whoever wants to become great among you must be your servant, and whoever wants to be first must be your slave—just as the Son of Man did not come to be served, but to serve, and to give his life as a ransom for many." (Matt. 20:25-28)

Clearly his kingdom was to be very different from the kingdoms of this world. In the last twenty years or so, people in the church have spent much more time in conversation about God's kingdom.

Unfortunately, though, sometimes our conversation makes it sound less like what Jesus described and more like the kingdoms of this world—with militant words of "taking this city" or "taking back this nation," etc.

So, with these difficulties in mind, let's survey the Bible and come to an understanding of this amazing kingdom that Jesus demonstrated and proclaimed. We will begin by simply asking, "What is a kingdom?"

A kingdom can be simply defined as *a sphere of influence in which a king (or queen) rules.* Within his kingdom, whatever the king says, goes. In the beginning, God spoke this world into existence. Whatever he said, it happened. When he said, "Let there be light," light burst forth where everything had been "cloaked in darkness."

Because God created this earth, the earth was his kingdom and he was the king: "I am the Lord, your Holy One, Israel's Creator, your King" (Isa. 43:15). And he had a plan to involve us in his kingdom! While that opened some exciting opportunities, it also led to a problem for all of creation! We will see this as we endeavor to understand two kingdoms—the kingdom of God and the kingdom of this world.

UNDERSTANDING TWO KINGDOMS

The diagram below consists of seven simple lines, two horizontal and five vertical.[1] Yet, if we understand the realities represented by these lines, we have a solid framework for understanding the whole of Scripture—and we'll see the concept of God's kingdom is integrated into the entire Biblical account. Virtually all of Scripture can be hung on this skeleton. Many heresies have seeped into the church over the centuries, because people have rushed to particular passages of Scripture without taking time to get the big picture. As we see the big picture, we find that God's kingdom is a central theme.

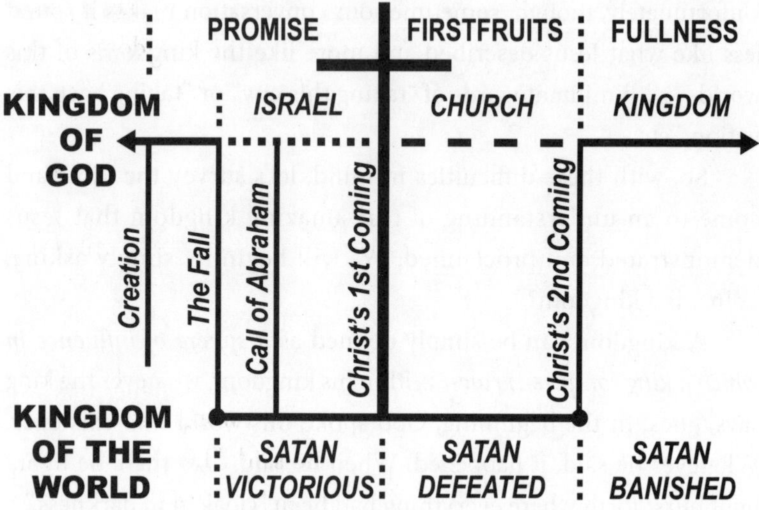

In this diagram, the two horizontal lines represent the kingdom of God and "the kingdom of the world" (Rev. 11:15). The top line represents the kingdom of God. Its arrows on both ends indicate a kingdom with neither beginning nor end. As Scripture says, "Your kingdom is an everlasting kingdom, and your dominion endures through all generations" (Ps. 145:13).

The lower line, with a definite beginning and end, symbolizes the kingdom of this world. All the fragmented kingdoms of humanity are included in this bottom line (see Rev. 11:15, Matt. 4:8).

The five vertical lines represent key historical events, four that have already happened and one that is yet to come. Let's look at each vertical line and see what they tell us about the two horizontal ones.

CREATION

Life as God Designed It

The Bible begins simply with these words: "In the beginning God created the heavens and the earth." In this very first verse, we see the integration of a spiritual world and a physical one: "God is spirit"

(John 4:24), and he created the physical universe that now stands as a general revelation of his character and purpose.

In the Bible's first two chapters, we see two complementary pictures of this creation. In the first chapter, which covers all of creation, we see the all-powerful God who simply spoke his will and brought this world into existence. The second chapter, focusing on the human race as creation's crown, shows an all-loving God who is intimately involved with these humans and their environment.

A friend of mine sees these chapters as pictures of the "Most High God" and the "Most Nigh God."[2] The God who says, "As the heavens are higher than the earth, so are my ways higher than your ways and my thoughts than your thoughts" (Isa. 55:9), is *also* "a friend who sticks closer than a brother" (Prov. 18:24).

Just as people throughout history have found it difficult to keep the spiritual world and the physical world integrated into one whole, so have they found it difficult to keep these two pictures of God together and balanced. At times, they have seen only the "Most High God," one awesome and all-powerful—but too distant to be involved in the everyday affairs of the human race. At other times they have seen only the "Most Nigh God," losing sight of his awesome majesty, seeing God only as a cosmic buddy whom they beckoned to do their bidding. Both are distortions of reality. Only as we hold these two pictures together do we have a healthy understanding of *the God who is there.*

A Fourfold Harmony of Relationships

In the Genesis account, we find Adam and Eve living fully under God's reign or rule. Thus, their experience is a good picture of life in the kingdom of God. We see a fourfold harmony of relationships—with God, self, others, and creation.

Clearly, Adam was familiar with "the sound of the LORD God as he was walking in the garden in the cool of the day" (Gen. 3:8). This shows a close, intimate relationship between God and the humans he created. God saw that it was "not good for the man to be alone," and he created Eve as a helper. This gave rise to the joy of close interpersonal relationships. (Gen. 2:18,24). They also were at peace within themselves, as "they were naked, and they felt no shame" (Gen. 2:25). They had nothing to hide.

Finally, the setting into which they were placed was a garden, a beautiful place filled with vegetation and animals. The physical creation itself was a place of harmony. We see no sign of conflict between animals, nor between animals and humans.

This fourfold harmony of relationships is perhaps the best definition we can give for the Hebrew word *shalom*. This beautiful word is usually translated as *peace*, but it means much more than that. It is a description of life lived fully in God's kingdom—a picture of spiritual, emotional, social, and physical harmony. This is an integrated life that holds together. This is the kind of life for which we were created.

A Four-Fold Responsibility

Genesis 1:28 notes that God blessed Adam and Eve and told them, "Be fruitful and increase in number, fill the earth and subdue it. Rule over the fish of the sea and the birds of the air and over every living creature that moves on the ground." Combine that passage with Genesis 2:15, which says, "The LORD God took the man and put him in the Garden of Eden to work it and take care of it." From these references, we see that God gave a fourfold responsibility to the human race.

First, we were to "fill the earth." We were created male and female to marry and establish families, filling the earth with our offspring.

Second, we were given responsibility to "subdue" or develop the earth—to bring out the potential that God had created into it. Science has been a great tool for bringing out this potential. It's sobering, however, to realize this potential can be used for good or for evil, depending upon our choices. For instance, we have developed the process of nuclear fission, which can produce either electrical power or weapons of mass destruction.

Third, God entrusted this good earth into our hands and said, "Rule over it!" The human race was the crown of God's creation, and God's desire was for us to partner with him in ruling the rest of it.

In creating us with free will—the right, ability, and responsibility to make our own decisions—God essentially gave each of us a "kingdom." We each make decisions every day about how we will live. In our work or ministry, we also may "rule" areas where our decisions are final. Everything that falls within our sphere of influence—that realm where we have responsibility and legitimate right to make decisions—is part of our "kingdom."

Dallas Willard has pointed out that having a "kingdom" is at the heart of our own personhood.[3] God created us as spiritual beings and gave us ability and freedom to make decisions about our own lives. This is what sets apart humans from the rest of God's creation, and it is the essence of personhood. "So God created human beings in his own image, in the image of God he created them; male and female he created them" (Gen. 1:27). Nothing remotely close to this is said about any other part of God's creation.

Nothing destroys our sense of personhood more than when another person violates our free will by controlling and manipulating us to do his or her will rather than our own. God, who gave us free will, does not violate our "kingdom." Neither should anyone else!

But we need to add a couple of qualifiers here. Parents of minor children have the legitimate right to make decisions that are beyond their children's level of maturity. But even here, parents are wise to give safe boundaries and allow their children to make decisions within those boundaries. When children arrive at adulthood, they need to know how to make wise decisions, not how to find someone else to make decisions for them.

Also, God ordained the state to maintain order when people refuse to act orderly (Rom. 13:1-5). Persons who violate the law and end up in prison surrender the right to make a lot of their own decisions. However, both in this case and in the case of minor children, they still retain the right to decide for or against cooperation with their guardians. If they choose not to cooperate, they must accept the consequences, for we all must learn that our decisions have consequences.

Finally, with regard to our four-fold responsibility, we were charged with cultivating and caring for this earth. As we rule over this earth, we must remember that we do not own it; we steward it. We are to treat it with respect and take care of it.

Adam and Eve had great freedom in carrying out these responsibilities, but not unlimited freedom. Only in submitting their "kingdoms" to the reigning authority of Yahweh God would they be competent to reign with him. Only God has the knowledge and perspective to fully determine what is good and what is evil. This is why, in the creation story, the "tree of the knowledge of good and evil" was off limits to Adam and Eve (Gen. 2:16,17).[4]

In our diagram, we see only the top horizontal line at this point. The created world and the kingdom of God are still one and the same—integrated. Thus the creation accounts are important to our understanding of God's kingdom, because they describe life as God designed it, before it was torn apart by sin. As we will see later, they also portray what life will one day be again, and the goal towards which things should be moving for Christians today.

THE FALL

Life Torn Apart

In his ground-breaking 1983 book on the subject of evil, Psychiatrist M. Scott Peck wrote:

> Five years ago when I began work on this book, I could no longer avoid the issue of the demonic.... Is there such a thing as evil spirit? Namely, the devil?
>
> I thought not. In common with 99 percent of psychiatrists and the majority of clergy, I did not think the devil existed.... I now know Satan is real. I have met it.[5]

On the Friday after 9/11, I found myself away from home, not wanting to be, and glued to the TV every free moment. In one of those moments, I heard a news anchor say, "We have to rethink our whole view of the world. There really is evil in the world!"

Indeed, in modern culture, the reality of evil slipped from the contemporary understanding of the world. Life was good, and human reason would always produce progress. But 9/11 raised new questions. How could this happen? How could people deliberately kill thousands of innocent people? Isn't that evil? To understand this dilemma, we turn to the third chapter of Genesis.

At this point in the Biblical story, two things happened: Another character entered the picture—and everything fell apart! A serpent came on the scene, identified later as "that ancient serpent called the devil, or Satan, who leads the whole world astray" (Rev. 12:9):

> Now the serpent was more crafty than any of the wild animals the LORD God had made. He said to the woman, "Did God really say, 'You must not eat from any tree in the garden'?"
>
> The woman said to the serpent, "We may eat fruit from the trees in the garden, but God did say, 'You must not eat fruit from the tree that is in the middle of the garden, and you must not touch it, or you will die.'"
>
> "You will not certainly die," the serpent said to the woman. "For God knows that when you eat of it your eyes will be opened, and you will be like God, knowing good and evil." (Gen. 3:1-4)

The devil's strategy hasn't changed. First, he loves to raise doubts in people's minds about what God has said: "Did God really say...." Second, he tells an outright lie, contradicting God: "You will *not* certainly die!" Finally, he tempts people to live independently of God, the Sin behind the sins, the root that bears all kinds of bad fruit: "Your eyes will be opened, and *you will be like God*, knowing good and evil."

This was the same idea that got Satan removed from God's presence in the first place. While the origins of Satan are somewhat obscure, a few Old Testament passages seem to address this, including Isaiah 14:12-15. Evidently Satan was one of the chief angels in God's presence, and he wanted to take God's place, so he rebelled:

> How you have fallen from heaven, morning star, son of the dawn! You have been cast down to the earth, you who once laid low the nations!
>
> You said in your heart, "*I will* ascend to heaven; *I will* raise my throne above the stars of God; *I will* sit enthroned on the mount of assembly, on the utmost heights of Mount Zaphon. *I will* ascend above the tops of the clouds; *I will* make myself like the Most High."
>
> But you are brought down to the realm of the dead, to the depths of the pit. (Emphasis added)

Note the five occurrences of "I will" in the second paragraph. *The essence of evil is to assert one's own will without regard for God or for the well-being of others.* We usually think of this as a violent thing—but it need not be. Sometimes it is just polite disregard for God's desires. The slide into rebellion can begin very subtly, but the result of rebellion against God is always the same, as Eugene Peterson so vividly captures in his biblical paraphrase:

> What happened was this: People knew God perfectly well, but when they didn't treat him like God, refusing to worship him, they trivialized themselves into silliness and confusion so that there was neither sense nor direction left in their lives. They pretended to know it all, but were illiterate regarding life. (Rom. 1:21,22 *THE MESSAGE*).

People may have a lot of knowledge, yet lack moral discernment. Their path will lead them farther and farther away from God, often into very degrading things. How many times have very gifted and talented people forfeited their destiny and ended up in disgrace, because they were unable to properly rule their own lives?

Discord Instead of Harmony

The results of rebellion against God were devastating. Harmony became discord—spiritually, emotionally, socially, and physically. Instead of enjoying a walk in the cool of the day, Adam and Eve hid from God (Gen. 3:8). Emotionally, shame entered the world, along with attempts to cover ourselves (Gen. 3:7). Instead of social harmony, the "blame game" started as Adam blamed Eve, and Eve blamed the serpent (Gen. 3:11-13). Physically, the garden's beauty and tranquility gave way to pain, sweat, thistles, and thorns (Gen. 3:16-19). The way to the Tree of Life was barred (Gen. 3:23,24). There would be no easy way back. It would cost Jesus his life to re-open the way.

A World in Bondage

Because of the Fall, the dominion given to humanity in creation ended up in Satan's hands. In the Gospel of Luke, we see Satan tempting Jesus by taking him to a high place and showing him all the world's kingdoms: "I will give you all their authority and splendor; *it has been given to me,* and I can give it to anyone I want to" (Luke 4:5,6, emphasis added). That's what happened at the Fall—dominion was handed over to the devil when Adam and Eve chose to listen to him rather than to God. John recognized this in his words, "We know that we are children of God, and that the whole world is under the control of the evil one" (1 John 5:19).

On the diagram, the lower horizontal line begins at this point. In the Fall, there was a terrible rending. Adam and Eve were cast from the garden into the everyday toil among the thistles. They had received freedom of choice from the Creator, and they exercised that choice by turning their backs upon God, determined to live according to their will rather than God's.

They were removed from the garden containing the Tree of Life, because this is not the way to life—it is the way of death! They moved from the kingdom of God to the kingdom of this world, to the kingdom of self, under Satan's dominion. It wasn't—and still isn't—a good place to be.

This alienation was the beginning of the difficulty in keeping life integrated, the root cause of fragmentation in our lives today. Ever since Adam and Eve chose their own way over God's, humanity has lived in a fallen condition, alienated from God and from each other. Humanity was separated from God and would stay that way until God took initiative to restore what had been lost.

Why Free Will?

The question is often asked at this point, "If God knew these consequences of our bad choices, why would he give us such freedom to begin with? Why not create us so we would automatically obey him?"

The answer is found in God's character: "God is love" (1 John 4:16). Love is at the center of who God is. And love does not exist without an object. We love someone or some thing. God created us in his image to be the object of his love. He wanted to have a meaningful, loving relationship with us.

God also understood that our relationships have meaning only as we choose to love. A child's relationship with his or her parents is a fact of biology. But biology alone does not give meaning to that relationship. It is the choice to express love that gives meaning! As a biological parent, foster parent, adoptive parent, and grandparent, I have experienced this reality many times!

ABRAHAM AND ISRAEL

Beginning Redemptive History

God is a redemptive God, not a vindictive one. He immediately declared he would frustrate Satan's schemes and redeem his fallen world. He promised that, while Satan would bruise the heel of the woman's offspring, that offspring would crush Satan's head (Gen.3:14,15). We will see that he was pointing to Jesus.

God created the human race because he wanted a loving relationship with us. He also chose to work out his purposes in this earth *through people!* Think about that: God, who had the power to speak this world into existence, could certainly have chosen to work in other ways, but he didn't. Invariably, when God wants to accomplish something in this earth, he looks for a person.

Blessed to Be a Blessing

When he was ready to initiate his redeeming and restoring work—putting this fragmented and alienated world back together—God found a willing vessel named Abram. He called Abram, promising a blessing, so that Abram could be a blessing to others:

> I will make you into a great nation and I will bless you; I will make your name great, and you will be a blessing.
>
> I will bless those who bless you, and whoever curses you I will curse; and all peoples on earth will be blessed through you. (Gen. 12:1-3).

Abram was faithful to the call, and God truly made him into a great nation. God even changed his name from Abram, meaning "exalted father," to Abraham, meaning "father of many." I will never forget my first trip to Israel, especially a visit to a small Arab village near the Sea of Galilee. We formed a circle, along with the Arab children of the village and our Jewish guide, and taught them the "Father Abraham" children's song:

> Father Abraham had many sons
> Many sons had Father Abraham
> I am one of them, and so are you
> So let's just praise the Lord!

Here, Arab children (sons of Abraham through Ishmael), a Jew (a son of Abraham through Isaac), and American Christians (adopted sons and daughters of Abraham, according to Gal. 3:7 and Eph. 1:5) all joined hands in a circle to honor a man who simply answered God's call and obeyed.

Later, this same call was given to Abraham's descendants, the nation of Israel, following their deliverance from slavery in Egypt:

> You yourselves have seen what I did to Egypt, and how I carried you on eagles' wings and brought you to myself. Now if you obey me fully and keep my covenant, then out of all nations you will be my treasured possession. Although the whole earth is mine, you will be for me a kingdom of priests and a holy nation. These are the words you are to speak to the Israelites. (Ex. 19:4-6).

For years, Israel lived with God as their king. But following the deaths of Moses and Joshua, their zeal for God waned. They eventually came to live more in the kingdom of the world than in the kingdom of God: "In those days there was no king in Israel; everyone did what was right in his own eyes" (Judg. 17:6, NLT). Reaping the consequences of self-centered living, they spent more time in bondage to neighboring nations than in freedom.

We Want a King Like Our Neighbors!

Tiring of this bondage, their solution was to ask for a king like their neighbors had, rather than to return to the kingdom of God (1 Sam. 8:1-9). The Prophet Samuel was not happy with their request, and took it to the Lord. The Lord responded: "Listen to all that the people are saying to you; *it is not you they have rejected, but they have rejected me as their king*" (1 Sam. 8:7, emphasis added). God warned them of the consequences, and then allowed them to have their king.

With few exceptions, from that point on, Israel's history shows the kings leading the people astray, and God sending prophets to call them back to obedience (Amos 7:10-17). Their experience of God's kingdom was incomplete and imperfect, represented by the dotted top line of the diagram.

A Time of Promise

Thankfully, God's prophets also pointed forward to a new day when God would act decisively on behalf of his people, a day when the kingdom would come in a new way. It was a time of PROMISE:

> "This is the covenant I will make with the house of Israel after that time," declares the LORD. I will put my law in their minds and write it on their hearts. I will be their God, and they will be my people. No longer will they teach their neighbors, or say to one another, 'Know the LORD,' because they will all know me, from the least of them to the greatest," (Jer. 31:33-34)

Understanding Abraham's call is essential to understanding the kingdom of God, as it is the beginning of redemptive history. "Blessed to be a blessing" was the call to Abraham, and to all who would follow in his footsteps. This is what the kingdom of God is about today, being set free from bondage to oneself to serve Christ and his kingdom, and to cooperate with God in carrying out his purposes.

CHRIST'S FIRST COMING—SALVATION

Firstfruits of Restoration

After a long spiritual drought in Israel, the time of fulfillment came. "But when the set time had fully come, God sent his Son, born of a woman, born under the law, to redeem those under the law, that we might receive adoption to sonship." (Gal. 4:4,5).

The Life of Jesus

Sometimes we rush too quickly over the life of Christ, finding significance only in his death and resurrection. But his life was important as well, for he revealed God's character: "Anyone who has seen me has seen the Father" (John 14:9). His life also demonstrated what life in the kingdom of God looks like—a fully integrated life.

We have already defined a kingdom as *a sphere of influence in which a king rules.* Therefore, wherever God rules we find an expression of his kingdom. We have also seen that Israel's experience was a limited and incomplete expression of God's kingdom, as the people walked sometimes in obedience to God, but often in disobedience.

With Jesus, a new expression of the kingdom was present on this earth, reflected in our diagram by the dotted line changing to a dashed line. He walked in *complete* obedience to his Father God. He came declaring, "I have come down from heaven not to do my will but to do the will of him who sent me" (John 6:38). He was so tuned to his Father that he could say, "the Son can do nothing by himself; he can do only what he sees his Father doing, because whatever the Father does the Son also does" (John 5:19). Further, "I do nothing on my own but speak just what the Father has taught me" (John 8:28). This is why he called his followers with the words, "Come, follow me!" He walked in front of them and set the pattern for obedience.

As he "did what he saw the Father doing," the power of God's kingdom was released in his life and ministry. When John the Baptist sat discouraged in prison, he sent some of his followers to ask of Jesus, "Are you the one who was to come, or should we expect someone else?" Jesus' reply was, "Go back and report to John what you have seen and heard: The blind receive sight, the lame walk, those who have leprosy are cleansed, the deaf hear, the dead are raised, and the good news is proclaimed to the poor" (Luke 7:20-22). He made a direct connection between God's power and the kingdom when he was accused of casting out demons by Beelzebub, the prince of demons: "If I drive out demons by the finger of God, then the kingdom of God has come upon you" (Luke 11:20).

Whenever the power of God is released in God's kingdom, it moves people away from the brokenness and fragmentation of the world in which they live, towards the wholeness of the kingdom of God. Jesus said, "The thief comes only to steal and kill and destroy; I have come that they may have life, and have it to the full" (John 10:10).

Through his life and ministry, Jesus also called out the first church. From among those who responded to his message, Jesus called twelve for a special role. He didn't take this lightly, but rather, the night before he chose them, he "went out to a mountainside to pray, and spent the night praying to God" (Luke 6:12). The next morning, he called his disciples to him and chose twelve of them, designating them apostles—meaning "ones sent out on a mission."

Jesus devoted most of his remaining earthly ministry to these twelve, and especially to the inner circle of Peter, James, and John. As the twelve sons of Jacob (great grandsons of Abraham) were the founding fathers of the tribes of Old Testament Israel, so these twelve would play a similar foundational role for the New Testament Church. After his resurrection and return to heaven, they would see the church established in the power of the Holy Spirit.

The Death and Resurrection of Jesus

While the life of Jesus was important for the reasons we have just noted, without his death and resurrection we would still be stuck in our sins and in our broken and fragmented lives. Jesus' death and resurrection broke Satan's hold upon this earth and opened the doorway into the kingdom of God.

As Jesus came to the latter days of his ministry, his attention turned to Jerusalem and all that would happen there. He was very clear with the disciples:

> "We are going up to Jerusalem," he said, "and the Son of Man will be delivered over to the chief priests and the teachers of the law. They will condemn him to death and will hand him over to the Gentiles, who will mock him and spit on him, flog him and kill him. Three days later he will rise." (Mark 10:33,34)

When he arrived in Jerusalem, things went just as Jesus said they would. He was falsely accused, arrested, tried, convicted and sentenced to crucifixion. As Jesus hung on the cross, I'm sure Satan thought he had won, eliminating this threat to his kingdom. I'm also sure that one second after the resurrection, he was aware that not only had he *not* won, he had actually just sealed his own fate!

> Since the children have flesh and blood, he *(Jesus)* too shared in their humanity so that by his death he might break the power of him who holds the power of death—that is, the devil—and free those who all their lives were held in slavery by their fear of death. (Heb. 2:14,15)

Jesus defeated Satan by dealing with the sin problem of the human race that had separated them from God and resulted in the fractured, fragmented, and frazzled lives we live. Paul sums this up well in his second letter to the Corinthian church:

> If anyone is in Christ, the new creation has come: The old has gone, the new is here! All this is from God, who reconciled us to himself through Christ and gave us the ministry of reconciliation: that God was reconciling the world to himself in Christ, not counting people's sins against them ... God made him who had no sin to be a sin offering[6] for us, so that in him we might become the righteousness of God. (2 Cor. 5:17-21)

In our world today, where being politically correct is often more important than understanding truth, many people have a problem with Jesus' death on the cross. Episcopalian Bishop John Spong has stated, "The view of the cross as the sacrifice for the sins of the world is a barbarian idea based on primitive concepts of God and must be dismissed."[7] In a CBS *60 Minutes* interview, speaking of Jesus dying for our sins, he added, "Let me tell you, I don't believe that. I think it's grotesque ... Why didn't God simply say, 'I forgive you'?"[8]

Why *did* Jesus need to die? Why *couldn't* God have simply said to the human race, "I forgive you"? In chapter one, I mentioned a woman who beat her four-year-old stepdaughter to death. What if her judge told her, "It's okay, I have decided to forgive you. You are free to go." What if there were no consequences—in this life or the life to come—for all those who have molested and murdered innocent children? What if there simply were no consequences for all the ways that people harm one another?

The thought of a world with no consequences is abhorrent to anyone not totally deceived by the devil. It would be an unjust world. What does it mean to be just? It is being "honorable and fair in one's dealings and actions...consistent with what is morally right; righteous... Properly due or merited... Valid within the law; lawful... suitable or proper in nature; fitting.... Based on fact or sound reason; well-founded."[9]

But unless there is a just God to give his standard of what is morally right, then who determines what is "honorable, fair, valid, suitable, or proper?" If we begin with fundamental assumptions that God does not exist, or that he does not give standards of morality and justice, then it should not be surprising that Bishop Spong and many others see no reason for Jesus' death.

Biblically, the Sin behind all sins is our desire to live independently of God, doing our own thing. A sinful attitude of rebellion against God leads to sinful actions. The predominant New Testament word for "sin" is *hamartia*, meaning "to miss the mark." To sin is to miss the mark that God has established.

But if there were no just God, how would we rebel against him? And if there were no standards, how could we miss the mark? And so, those who embrace these assumptions would see no need for atonement, and the idea of Jesus dying on the cross would indeed be a grotesque idea.

But if there is a real, just and moral God who has revealed in history what is right and wrong, and if we have all done wrong, or missed the mark, as Romans 3:23 declares, then there must be consequences—someone must pay. That's what Jesus did for us.

One last point here: some people say that if God required an innocent Jesus to die for us, that would itself be an unjust action. And, indeed, *if* God had required Jesus to die *against his will*, he would have violated the free will God has given to every person. That would have been an unjust action. However, that is not the case. Jesus said, "I lay down my life ... No one takes it from me, but I lay it down of my own accord" (John 10:17,18).

Earlier in this chapter we saw that the essence of evil was to assert one's own will without regard for God or for the wellbeing of others. Here we see the essence of the good—to submit one's own will to God's for the wellbeing of others.

This was and is the supreme act of love that stands as the climax in the drama of world history! What remains is the denouement—the final outcome of that victory over evil, played out before our eyes. Better yet, we get to participate in the denouement as we fulfill the part assigned to us by God himself.

The Era of Firstfruits

With his life, death and resurrection, Jesus paid the price of sin and defeated Satan, breaking the devil's hold on all of creation. In so doing, he opened the door to a new day in the kingdom of God, a day of FIRSTFRUITS. The kingdom of God was here in a new way, yet not in its fullness.

This is the time in which we now live. Having raised him from the dead, Acts 2:36 declares that God has now "made Jesus both Lord and Christ." Recognizing God as king and living in his kingdom simply requires that we place our faith and trust in Jesus as Savior and Lord, by way of God's grace to us (Eph.2:8,9). Those who receive

Jesus as Savior and Lord make up the church. Local churches become "outposts of the kingdom." That phrase is not original with me, but I no longer remember where it came from, and do not know whom to credit. It is one of my favorite definitions of the church.

Those who are now "in Christ" have established their citizenship in the kingdom of God: "For he has rescued us from the dominion of darkness and brought us into the kingdom of the Son he loves" (Col. 1:13). We have a whole new set of possibilities before us. We have a new source of life—the Holy Spirit (Acts 1:4-8; Gal. 5:13-18). We live a new lifestyle of love (Matt. 22:34-40; John 13:34,35). With our new Lord comes a new occupation—we are ambassadors of the King (1 Cor. 6:19,20; 2 Cor. 5:16-21).

For believers, life should become an ever-increasing experience of God's kingdom. We "are being transformed into his image with ever-increasing glory..." (2 Cor.3:18). As this occurs, we also enjoy an ever-increasing experience of *shalom*, that fourfold harmony of relationships seen in the garden.

We also bring the values of the kingdom of God—love, righteousness, justice, peace, faith, and joy—to others in our sphere of influence. Fractured and frazzled lives become more integrated. The restoration has begun!

This experience, however, is incomplete. While the kingdom of God was fully present in Jesus and is currently present in the Holy Spirit, our obedience to the Spirit is not perfect. Consequently, like Israel, our experience of the kingdom is imperfect and incomplete. Even as we grow in our relationship with God and in our obedience to his truth, we wait eagerly for something else (Eph. 1:14; Rom. 8:22-25).

Citizens of Two Kingdoms

In this time between Christ's first and second comings, we carry a dual citizenship. We are already citizens of the kingdom of God, yet we still live on an earth that is under the curse of sin. We are very much like the children of Israel after Mount Sinai but before the

Promised Land. Because of their disobedience, they wandered in the desert, known as the "Wilderness of Sin," for forty years before entering the Promised Land. Likewise, we have established our citizenship in the kingdom of God, but still live physically in the midst of a similar "wilderness of sin." Satan has been defeated, but is not yet banished.

This present age is a time of continuing conflict between these two kingdoms. Although Satan has been defeated, he still retains dominion over much of creation through deception and intimidation. He knows that his time is short, is "filled with fury," and has "blinded the minds of unbelievers" (2 Cor. 4:4). Even against those who have put their faith in Jesus, he has not given up the fight. He "makes war against ... those who obey God's commands and hold fast their testimony about Jesus" (Rev.12:17).

But he will not succeed! The Church will declare in word and deed the glory of the kingdom of God, prevailing against him (Matt. 16:18)! We will depend on God's power to remove the strongholds that Satan has put in our way and to bring change into our world. As the Apostle Paul wrote in 2 Corinthians 10:4-5:

> For though we live in the world, we do not wage war as the world does. The weapons we fight with are not the weapons of the world. On the contrary, they have divine power to demolish strongholds. We demolish arguments and every pretension that sets itself up against the knowledge of God, and we take captive every thought to make it obedient to Christ.

CHRIST'S SECOND COMING—JUDGMENT

Restoration in Fullness

The evil and injustice of this present age will one day give way to the justice of Almighty God. A new day is coming, the age of FULLNESS. When Jesus returns, this present world will give way to a new one: "The kingdom of the world has become the kingdom of our Lord and of his Christ, and he will reign for ever and ever" (Rev. 11:15). The lower horizontal line in our diagram comes to an end!

Those who have refused to come to Jesus will receive the only appropriate consequence of their decision: they will be banished forever from God's presence (Rev. 20:10-15). This is another reality that many people today have problems with: "How could a loving God send someone to hell?" they ask.

God does not send anyone to hell—he actually has opened a way to avoid it. For those who refuse to acknowledge God and live in his presence today, would it be right to force them to spend eternity with God? Would it not be respecting their free will to let them experience in eternity what they have chosen throughout their earthly lives—to be separated from God?

Believers, on the other hand, will be received into a new world, into the fullness of life as God intended from the beginning. At this point, everything God has promised will be experienced in complete fulfillment. God will reign supreme, and *shalom* will be the order of his kingdom! (Rev. 21:1-7). The way to the tree of life will again be wide open (Rev. 22:12-14)!

The conclusion of the matter has been well summed up by George Eldon Ladd:

> And so the Bible ends, with a redeemed society dwelling on a new earth that has been purged of all evil, with God dwelling in the midst of His people. This is the goal of the long course of redemptive history.[10]

This "big story of the kingdom" gives us an overall picture of the kingdom of God. Now we are ready to look more closely at what Jesus and the early church called the "good news."

APPLICATION TO LIFE

1. What do you think when you hear that you have a "kingdom?" What does your kingdom look like? What or who is included in your rightful sphere of influence? On what do you base the decisions that you make within your kingdom?

2. Has anyone ever tried to make decisions that rightly belonged to you? How does that feel? Have you ever done this to others?

3. The Bible begins with the words "In the beginning God…" When you think of God, what comes to your mind? Where did you get this picture of God? Do you think it is an accurate picture?

4. When you think of Jesus returning some day, what thoughts are stirred up in your mind? Are they pleasant thoughts or disturbing ones?

4

THE GOSPEL OF THE KINGDOM

Because of his great love for us, God, who is rich in mercy,
made us alive with Christ even when we were dead
in transgressions—it is by grace you have been saved.
And God raised us up with Christ and seated us
with him in the heavenly realms in Christ Jesus...
(Eph. 2:4-6)

Recently I was driving and listening to a local Christian radio station, when someone requested "any song about soul-winning!" She had been talking to her pastor and was "all pumped up about winning souls for Jesus."

I appreciate her desire to share her faith. However, this language—used by many—reinforces the compartmentalized living we have been addressing. Jesus is not just interested in "winning souls" to go to heaven when they die, but he is calling to people, "Come! Follow me!" In this life—now!

He is interested in whole people relating to whole people, for now *and* for all eternity. When asked which commandment was most important, he responded:

> The most important one ... is this: "Hear, O Israel: The Lord our God, the Lord is one. Love the Lord your God with all your heart and with all your soul and with all your mind and with all your strength." The second is this: "Love your neighbor as yourself." There is no commandment greater than these. (Matt. 12:29-31).

With all your heart and soul and mind and strength—that sounds like *with your whole person.* Paul echoed this whole-person theme in his prayer for the Christians at Thessalonica:

> May God himself, the God who makes everything holy and whole, make you holy and whole, put you together—spirit, soul, and body—and keep you fit for the coming of our Master, Jesus Christ. The One who called you is completely dependable. If he said it, he'll do it! (1 Thess. 5:23-24, *THE MESSAGE*)

The gospel we present to people helps define their response. If we want people to "get saved" for heaven *and* to become mature and fruitful followers of Jesus who impact this world, that desire must be reflected in our words and actions. As my friend Ron Klaus says, "Whatever is not *explicit* in the gospel we present to people will always be considered *optional* by them." For example, if the gospel presentation calls only for praying the sinner's prayer, then becoming fully devoted followers of Jesus will be considered a nice option, but not part of the basic package.

So when we have opportunity to share the gospel with someone who is not yet Jesus' follower, what will we share? Well, I recommend this book! That is one of my main reasons for writing it. However, I know some occasions will not allow for sharing the entire book. This chapter is for those situations.

To begin, we must lay aside our preconceived ideas about "soul-winning" and return to the New Testament, to look afresh at the gospel found there—the integrating gospel that really is good news for all of life, now and forevermore!

The Good News Proclaimed by Jesus

In Chapter three we noted that Jesus' earthly ministry was based on the "gospel of the kingdom." Early in his ministry, Jesus stopped in the town of Capernaum. He healed sick people and freed those under demonic influence. The people of Capernaum were so thrilled, they tried to talk Jesus into staying with them. But Jesus was so focused on his mission, he resisted their pressure: "I must preach the good news of the kingdom of God to the other towns also, because that is why I was sent" (Luke 4:43).

Somewhat later "Jesus traveled about from one town and village to another, proclaiming the good news of the kingdom of God" (Luke 8:1). On one occasion as he was speaking about John the Baptist, he said, "The Law and the Prophets were proclaimed until John. Since that time, the good news of the kingdom of God is being preached, and people are forcing their way into it" (Luke 16:16).

When instructing his disciples how to pray, he gave a pattern:

> Our Father in heaven, hallowed be your name, *your kingdom come, your will be done on earth as it is in heaven.* Give us today our daily bread. Forgive us our debts, as we also have forgiven our debtors. And lead us not into temptation, but deliver us from the evil one. (Matt. 6:9-13, emphasis added).

Even as Jesus' earthly ministry drew to a close, just prior to his crucifixion, this message of God's kingdom was on his lips. As he ate the Last Supper with his disciples he said, "I have eagerly desired to eat this Passover with you before I suffer. For I tell you, I will not eat it again until it finds fulfillment in the kingdom of God" (Luke 22:15,16).

Then, after his resurrection, he shared his last 40 days on earth with those closest to him "and spoke about the kingdom of God" (Acts 1:3). From beginning to end, Jesus focused on this message that he called "the good news of the kingdom."

The Good News Proclaimed by the Church

What about the Church that was left behind when Jesus returned to heaven? Did they simply preach, "Jesus died for your sins?" Or, did they proclaim the same message as Jesus did?

In Acts 8:12, we read that Phillip "proclaimed the good news of the kingdom of God *and the name of Jesus Christ*" (emphasis added). Likewise, as we come to the end of the book of Acts, we find Paul a prisoner in Rome, yet free to welcome those who came to him. Even there Paul "proclaimed the kingdom of God and taught about the Lord Jesus Christ—with all boldness and without hindrance!" (Acts 28:31). In other words, both Phillip and Paul taught Jesus' message about God's kingdom. But now they added the role that Jesus' life, death, and resurrection played in this good news.

Virtually every New Testament writer proclaimed the kingdom. James wrote, "Has not God chosen those who are poor in the eyes of the world to be rich in faith and to inherit the kingdom he promised those who love him?" (James 2:5). Peter wrote that those who remain faithful "will receive a rich welcome into the eternal kingdom of our Lord and Savior Jesus Christ" (2 Pet. 1:11). The writer of Hebrews wrote that "since we are receiving a kingdom that cannot be shaken, let us be thankful, and so worship God acceptably with reverence and awe" (12:28). And in the final book of our Bible, as John recorded The Revelation, he described loud voices in heaven proclaiming, "The kingdom of the world has become the kingdom of our Lord and of his Messiah, and he will reign for ever and ever" (11:15).

Thus, from the beginning of Jesus' ministry through the end of the New Testament, this "good news of the kingdom" was central to the message. Indeed, Jesus clearly intended it to be central as long as this earth remains: "This gospel of the kingdom will be preached in the whole world as a testimony to all nations, and then the end will come" (Matt. 24:14).

So How Do We Proclaim it?

If the gospel of the kingdom was so important to Jesus and to the New Testament Church, shouldn't that be reflected in our gospel presentation today? As I have traveled widely throughout the American Church over the last 25 years, I have asked people "Tell me, what is the good news?" Almost without fail, they say, "Jesus died for my sins." And I say to them, "That is indeed good news, but it is not what Jesus and the early Church called *the* good news." Less than five percent of those responding to my question have mentioned anything about God's kingdom.

So, if we want to proclaim the gospel, where should we start? I suggest going to Paul's letter to the Ephesians. Perhaps no other passage has been used by evangelical Christians more frequently in presenting the gospel than Ephesians 2:8,9:

> For it is by grace you have been saved, through faith—and this not from yourselves, it is the gift of God—not by works, so that no one can boast.

These two verses contain very important truth. However, if used alone, they present an incomplete and even misleading gospel. In reality, when we read those verses in context of the entire letter to the Ephesians, we find a beautiful presentation of the gospel of the kingdom, particularly in the first two chapters. Based on Ephesians 1 and 2, we can define the good news of the kingdom in terms of four principles: *Purpose, Problem, Provision, People.*

PURPOSE

Definition:

> God is unifying all things in heaven and on earth under one head—Jesus. He has raised Jesus from the dead and seated him at his right hand, enabling his rule over every power, authority, and dominion.

Ephesians 1:

> With all wisdom and understanding, he made known to us the mystery of his will according to his good pleasure, which he purposed in Christ, to be put into effect when the times reach their fulfillment—to bring unity to all things in heaven and on earth under Christ….
>
> He raised Christ from the dead and seated him at his right hand in the heavenly realms, far above all rule and authority, power and dominion, and every name that can be invoked, not only in the present age but also in the one to come. And God placed all things under his feet and appointed him to be head over everything for the church, which is his body, the fullness of him who fills everything in every way. (1:8-10, 20-23)

This chapter clarifies God's plan. He is putting back together a fractured and fragmented world. But we need to highlight a specific word that shows up later in this chapter. Jesus is now "seated" at the Father's right hand. The significance is mostly lost in our day, but in ancient times, kings took their seat on a throne to rule. When they were seated, they embraced their position of authority. We still see this among Catholics, who believe the Pope is infallible when speaking "ex cathedra," meaning literally "from the chair."

From this seat, Jesus now reigns as the King of kings and Lord of lords (Heb. 12:2; Rev. 19:16). After Jesus completed his work of atonement through his death and resurrection, God established his Son as the Sovereign of his kingdom, above all other kingdoms. In this kingdom, God's restoring power will enable his followers to experience life as God intended from the beginning.

This will fully take place only when "the times reach their fulfillment." In the meantime, those who put our hope in Christ experience the firstfruits of this integrated and reconciled kingdom.

PROBLEM

Definition:

> We were alienated from God and his kingdom by our self-centered attitudes and lifestyles, and we were held in bondage to sin and Satan.

Ephesians 2:

> As for you, you were dead in your transgressions and sins, in which you used to live when you followed the ways of this world and of the ruler of the kingdom of the air, the spirit who is now at work in those who are disobedient. All of us also lived among them at one time, gratifying the cravings of our sinful nature and following its desires and thoughts. Like the rest, we were by nature deserving of wrath. (vs. 1-3)

It may seem strange to include a "problem" in a definition of "good news." But seldom do people seek a solution unless they recognize a problem. And they must understand the *nature* of the problem, or they will seek the wrong solution.

This is precisely the predicament of our Western culture. People typically think there's no problem, or they say, "The problem is with the system ... or with other people ... or the economy ... or the government ... or religious fanatics ... just anywhere else than with *me*!"

Both modern and postmodern cultures are human-centered. They largely dismiss God and his Word, concluding that the human self is the creative source of life and the ultimate authority. Modernists see the individual this way, while postmodernists see the collective self or community this way.

If we embrace these ideas, we place the problem *outside* ourselves. That's why we see a "victim mindset" just about everywhere—even sometimes in the Church. Remember the words of Alan Wolfe from an earlier chapter: "American faith has met American culture—and American culture has triumphed."[1]

Over the last 25 years, I've watched the focus of ministry move away from confession and repentance of sin, as required in the New Testament, and more towards "healing of past hurts." I realize the sins of others impact our lives in a negative way, and certainly, God offers healing.

But things are out of balance. Too often the victim mindset of our culture has been dressed up in spiritual terms so it can invade the Church. Tragically, this often proves to be a "different gospel that is really no gospel at all" (Gal. 1:7). It leaves people stuck in sin and dysfunction—looking in the wrong places for their solution.

The Root Problem

God's Word indicates that the Sin behind our sins—the root that bears bad fruit—is our desire to live independently of God, doing our own thing. And, Paul's words leave out no one: "All of us also lived among them at one time, gratifying the cravings of our sinful nature and following its desires and thoughts" (2:3). We have *all* followed in the footsteps of Adam and Eve, following the "ruler of the kingdom of the air, the spirit who is now at work in those who are disobedient." Paul writes in Romans that we were in such bondage that we were actually "slaves to sin" (6:17).

Similarly, Jesus acknowledged the existence of a thief who came "only to steal and kill and destroy." But Jesus came for a different purpose: "I have come that they may have life, and have it to the full" (John 10:10). To him, the way to this "life to the full" was not through self-fulfillment, self-actualization, or self-confidence; it was actually grounded in self-denial—releasing people from bondage to themselves, and freeing them to follow him and experience his kingdom:

> "Whoever wants to be my disciple must deny themselves and take up their cross daily and follow me. For whoever

> wants to save their life will lose it, but whoever loses their life for me will save it. What good is it for you to gain the whole world, and yet lose or forfeit your very self? (Luke 9:23-25)

When we stay broken and self-centered, life doesn't work well for us, and God cannot use us as agents of reconciliation for a fragmented world.

The Wrath of God

The last sentence in that Ephesians passage is hard to grasp in today's world: "We were by nature deserving of wrath." How can we reconcile God's love and his wrath? Paul gives insight in the first chapter of Romans: "The wrath of God *is* being revealed from heaven against all the godlessness and wickedness of human beings who suppress the truth by their wickedness" (v.18). This letter was written about A.D. 57. According to Paul, God's wrath was *then* being revealed in Rome. How was this happening? Were people being struck down by a plague or a similar divine punishment? Not that we have record of.

In the rest of Romans 1, Paul writes of the sinful attitudes and behaviors of that period. In this context, three times he writes that God "gave them over" (v.24,26,28). He gave them over to "sinful desires," to "shameful lusts," and ultimately to a "depraved mind."

God's wrath was revealed when he simply gave people over to the consequences of their own choices. They wanted to live independently of God; he allowed them to experience what that is like. The book of Proverbs notes, "The mouth of an adulterous woman is a deep pit; a man who is under the LORD's wrath falls into it" (Prov. 22:14). In other words, when people turn their backs on God, at some point he withdraws his mercy, and they experience the consequences of their sin.

Time for a Change

As we come to understand God's judgment, we need to ask ourselves some serious questions. Has our cultural focus on self brought more *shalom* into our lives—into our relationship with God, with ourselves, with others, or with the physical world? If not, maybe we should consider what the Bible says—that living in a self-focused way is the problem, not the solution!

PROVISION

Definition:

> In his love, mercy and grace, God sent Jesus to demonstrate kingdom-living, and to pay the penalty of our sin. Then he invited us to follow him, serving God and reigning with him in his kingdom.

Ephesians 2:

> But because of his great love for us, God, who is rich in mercy, made us alive with Christ even when we were dead in transgressions—it is by grace you have been saved. And God raised us up with Christ and seated us with him in the heavenly realms in Christ Jesus, in order that in the coming ages he might show the incomparable riches of his grace, expressed in his kindness to us in Christ Jesus. For it is by grace you have been saved, through faith—and this not from yourselves, it is the gift of God—not by works, so that no one can boast. For we are God's handiwork, created in Christ Jesus to do good works, which God prepared in advance for us to do. (vs. 4-10)

The God Who Pursues

The previous section gave the bad news about our condition apart from God. Unfortunately, like Adam and Eve, when we become aware of that separation, our first instinct is to hide. But even while we are hiding, God is pursuing us! A favorite song of mine from long ago expresses this good news:

> I sought the Lord, and afterward I knew
> He moved my soul to seek him, seeking me;
> It was not I that found, O Savior true,
> No, I was found of Thee.[2]

Human rebellion in the Garden ripped open the breach in our relationship with God. And immediately, God's love proclaimed his plan: One would be born of woman who would crush Satan and repair the breach, restoring the relationship. That One would be Jesus. His coming would be the climax of all history:

> But when the right time came, God sent his Son, born of a woman, subject to the law. God sent him to buy freedom for us who were slaves to the law, so that he could adopt us as his very own children. (Galatians 4:4,5, NLT)

Because I've adopted three children, I know the process. When we adopted our first child, the judge asked, "Do you understand that when I sign this order, Destinee will become your legal child and heir, with all the rights that come with that?"

When the judge signed the adoption order, Destinee became our daughter. Now, as her parents, we accepted responsibility to provide for her until she became an adult. In the same way, when God adopts us into his family, he provides for us. His provision includes love, mercy, grace, life, authority, and the capacity to reclaim our destiny!

Love

"But because of his great love for us..." Everything in God's kingdom flows from this. Love is not just what God does, but it's *who he is,* for John wrote: "God is love" (1 John 4:16). But love means different things to different people. So when we say "God is love," what are we saying? To answer that, we must go back to the original language.

The Greek language of the New Testament has three different words that are all translated as *love*. Let's start at the bottom and work our way up.

Eros is a selfish kind of love. If you *eros* someone, you want to use them for your own pleasure. People often think of *eros* as sexual love, as in erotic, but it is not necessarily sexual. Any time a person wants any kind of relationship solely for his or her own pleasure, that is *eros*. Interestingly enough, the Greek New Testament does not use *eros*. But it may be the most prevalent expression of love in our world today, given our extreme focus on self-fulfillment, self-actualization, etc.

The second kind of love is *phileo*, as in "Philadelphia, the city of brotherly love." This is a reciprocal kind of love, where the relationship benefits both parties. This kind of love is expressed in the Barney song that I sing to my little kids and my grandkids: "I love you, you love me, we're a happy family..." This is certainly different from *eros*.

The highest kind of love is *agape*, the word that is found in "God is love." *Agape* is the opposite of *eros*—it is selfless, not selfish. It is a sacrificial love, where persons give themselves on behalf of another, without regard for the return. This is the way God gave of himself, in sending Jesus to save us. The highest act of *agape* love this world has ever seen is expressed by Paul:

> At just the right time, when we were still powerless, Christ died for the ungodly. Very rarely will anyone die for a righteous person, though for a good person someone might possibly dare to die. *But God demonstrates his own love for us in this:* While we were still sinners, Christ died for us. (Rom. 5:6-8, emphasis added)

This is *agape*. This is God's love for us. It is the love that he *is*. And, since his Spirit lives within those who are Jesus' followers, we can love in the same way. In fact, Jesus said this would be the distinguishing mark of those who would follow him: "By this everyone will know that you are my disciples, if you love one another" (John 13:35). Paul describes what this would look like:

> Love is patient, love is kind. It does not envy, it does not boast, it is not proud. It does not dishonor others, it is not self-seeking, it is not easily angered, it keeps no record of wrongs. Love does not delight in evil but rejoices with the truth. It always protects, always trusts, always hopes, always perseveres. (1 Cor. 13:4-7)

This *agape* fuels God's kingdom, as we put it into practice in our everyday lives!

Mercy

God also is "rich in mercy," but before we can really understand this attribute, we first must understand his justice. The prophet Isaiah tells us, "The LORD Almighty will be exalted by his justice, and the holy God will be proved holy by his righteous acts" (Isaiah 5:16). Because our righteous God created a moral universe, sin has consequences. If justice doesn't prevail in this life, it will in eternity: "For he has set a day when he will judge the world with justice by the man he has appointed. He has given proof of this to all men by raising him from the dead" (Acts 17:31).

Scripture clearly says we are all guilty before God: "For all have sinned and fall short of the glory of God" (Rom. 3:23). *But in his mercy, God spares us from the judgment we deserve.* Because of his love he extends mercy, and "Mercy triumphs over judgment!" (James 2:13).

This does not mean God decided to overlook sin. He could extend mercy only because Jesus willingly gave himself on our behalf to satisfy God's justice:

> God presented him as a sacrifice of atonement, through faith in his blood. He did this to demonstrate his justice, because in his forbearance he had left the sins committed

> beforehand unpunished—he did it to demonstrate his justice at the present time, so as to be just and the one who justifies those who have faith in Jesus (Rom. 3:25).

People still must choose. They can embrace Jesus and accept his payment for their sin. Or, they can reject him—and pay the price themselves. One way or another, justice requires that the price be paid. Praise be to God for his mercy to us in Christ!

Grace

Mercy spares us the consequences we deserve. But God's love goes beyond even that. *In his grace God goes beyond mercy, giving us the good things we don't deserve:* "God ... made us alive with Christ even when we were dead in transgressions—it is by grace you have been saved." This saving grace comes to us "through faith—and this not from yourselves, it is the gift of God—not by works, so that no one can boast" (2:8,9). Even our ability to believe is a gift from God. As we simply turn from our running and embrace God in sincere humility, God births faith in our spirit. With that gift, we can take hold of the good news of the kingdom of God and the Lord Jesus.

We cannot earn salvation by our works; neither can we conjure up our own faith. Both are gifts from God. As we soften our hearts toward God, the Holy Spirit convicts us of sin, draws us to God, and pours out his gifts upon us as we embrace him and yield to his kingdom.

We must define grace carefully, lest we be misunderstood. Grace really is God's empowerment for change. But our culture has tainted our understanding of Biblical concepts, so that even Christians sometimes see grace as permission to stay the same.

Dietrich Bonhoeffer called that "cheap grace." He explained:

> Cheap grace means grace as a doctrine, a principle, a system. It means forgiveness of sins proclaimed as a general truth, the love of God taught as the Christian

> 'conception' of God. An intellectual assent to that idea is held to be of itself sufficient to secure remission of sins.... In such a Church the world finds a cheap covering for its sins; no contrition is required, still less any real desire to be delivered from sin. Cheap grace therefore amounts to a denial of the living Word of God, in fact, a denial of the Incarnation of the Word of God.
>
> Cheap grace means the justification of sin without the justification of the sinner.... Cheap grace is the grace we bestow on ourselves. Cheap grace is the preaching of forgiveness without requiring repentance, baptism without church discipline, Communion without confession.... Cheap grace is grace without discipleship, grace without the cross, grace without Jesus Christ, living and incarnate.
>
> Costly grace is the treasure hidden in the field; for the sake of it a man' will gladly go and sell all that he has. It is the pearl of great price to buy which the merchant will sell all his goods. It is the kingly rule of Christ, for whose sake a man will pluck out the eye which causes him to stumble, it is the call of Jesus Christ at which the disciple leaves his nets and follows him.[3]

This costly grace is not permission to stay in our sin; it is God's provision, empowering us to be transformed into Jesus' image.

Life

"God ... made us alive with Christ even when we were dead in transgressions" (2:5). Our old life, which was really more death than life, has been crucified with Christ, and God has given us the very life of Christ:

> I have been crucified with Christ and I no longer live, but Christ lives in me. The life I live in the body, I live by

> faith in the Son of God, who loved me and gave himself for me. (Gal. 2:20)

As a pastor, I have often heard Christians excuse some sin in their life by saying, "I'm only human."

My response is, "That's not quite true. You indeed are human. But you are not *just* human. You have the very life of God within you!"

When we truly grasp this, it begins to revolutionize our lives. We realize we don't have to stay where we have been stuck for so long. "Christ living in me" opens a whole new realm of possibilities.

This unfolding of new life is what Scripture calls *salvation*. And it involves much more than just being able to say "yes" when someone asks if you are "saved." Salvation clearly is a process, not a onetime event, as the Bible uses the word *saved* in all three tenses—past, present and future. Ralph W. Neighbour, Jr. points out:

> **PAST** - For it is by grace you *have been saved*, through faith—and this not from yourselves, it is the gift of God (Acts 2:8, emphasis added).
>
> We *have been saved* from the *penalty* of sin, as we have already passed from death to life
>
> **PRESENT** - For the message of the cross is foolishness to those who are perishing, but to us who *are being saved* it is the power of God. (1 Cor. 1:18, emphasis added).
>
> We *are being saved* from the *power* of sin, as its hold on us is being broken in an ever-increasing way as we yield ourselves to God and grow in our relationship and in our kingdom walk with him.
>
> **FUTURE** - Because of the increase of wickedness, the love of most will grow cold, but he who stands firm to the end *will be saved*. And this gospel of the kingdom will be preached in the whole world as a testimony to all nations, and then the end will come. (Matt. 24:12-14, emphasis added).

> We *will be saved* from the very *presence* of sin when Jesus returns and the kingdom of God comes in all its fullness.[4]

Freed from the past, alive and growing in the present, anticipating the future—this is the full scope of the life that Jesus offers!

Authority

Often people—especially evangelical Christians—treat Ephesians 2:6-7 as an unnecessary interlude between verses five and eight. I came across this again in the devotional program I am currently using:

> And God raised us up with Christ … in order that in the coming ages he might show the incomparable riches of his grace, expressed in his kindness to us in Christ Jesus. For it is by grace you have been saved, through faith—and this not from yourselves, it is the gift of God—not by works, so that no one can boast. (Eph. 2:6-9)[5]

The author or editor omitted these words: "and seated us with him in the heavenly realms in Christ Jesus." We noted that Jesus is now "seated" at God's right hand—the position of authority from which he rules his kingdom. These words are not just unimportant filler—they tell us that we share that position of authority! If we fail to understand this, we will miss a very important aspect of the gospel of the kingdom.

From this "seat of authority" we can now live a life victorious over all influences of evil. John wrote "The reason the Son of God appeared was to destroy the devil's work" (1 John 3:8). What is the devil's work? Jesus said it was "to steal and kill and destroy" the abundant life that Jesus offers. (John 10:10) Along with the authority (the right to do something) comes the power (the ability to do it), as we are empowered to live this victorious life by "the promised Holy Spirit" (Eph 1:13).

Destiny

God seated us there for a purpose: "For we are God's handiwork, created in Christ Jesus to do good works, which God prepared in advance for us to do" (2:10). We are saved *from* our sins and *for* the kingdom!

This is not just a picture of something to be realized in the future; it is a *present* reality that can change our present-day lives. As we submit our kingdoms to his, we can *now* see order and purpose restored to our lives. God has restored our competency to reign with Christ.

God's plan has always been to work through his people to bring blessing to his world. We share Abraham's calling—we are "blessed to be a blessing." As our kingdoms align under God's, "the incomparable riches of his grace" are expressed in his kindness to us. Then we pass it on to others.

We begin to live a different life—one that looks more like Jesus' example. We love as he loved, serve as he served, forgive as he forgave, and administer healing as he healed. Beginning with our own lives and spreading throughout our sphere of influence, we can see our lives and the lives of others become more integrated and whole. As reconciled daughters and sons of God, we become ambassadors of reconciliation to the rest of the world (2 Cor. 5:18-21).

Love, mercy, grace, life, authority, destiny—such are God's provisions for his adopted children. As Peter writes, "His divine power has given us everything we need for life and godliness" (2 Pet. 1:3, NIV).

PEOPLE

Definition:

Those who respond become one new body, experiencing his peace and being built together as a dwelling in which God lives by his Spirit.

Ephesians 2:

> But now in Christ Jesus you who once were far away have been brought near by the blood of Christ. For he himself is our peace, who has made the two one and has destroyed the barrier, the dividing wall of hostility... His purpose was to create in himself one new humanity out of the two, thus making peace, and in one body to reconcile both of them to God through the cross, by which he put to death their hostility. (vs. 13-16)
>
> Consequently, you are no longer foreigners and strangers, but fellow citizens with God's people and also members of his household, built on the foundation of the apostles and prophets, with Christ Jesus himself as the chief cornerstone. In him the whole building is joined together and rises to become a holy temple in the Lord. And in him you too are being built together to become a dwelling in which God lives by his Spirit. (vs. 19-22)

Someone once told me that Christianity is personal, but it is not private. The Holy Spirit takes our individual "provinces" and molds them into one body. As we are reconciled to God, this reconciliation spills over into relationships with others, destroying the hostility that has kept us apart.

As this happens, we see what God is up to—he is building "one new humanity out of two." In this context, Paul is describing how Jewish people and gentiles become one new family in Christ. But John tells us this new humanity will include "members of every tribe and language and people and nation" who will be "a kingdom and priests to serve our God, and they will reign on the earth" (Rev. 5:9,10).

As we are united, we become "a holy temple in the Lord ... a dwelling in which God lives by his Spirit" (Eph. 2:21,22).

Reconciliation to God and reconciliation to each other fulfills the Great Commandment:

> Love the Lord your God with all your heart and with all your soul and with all your mind." This is the first and greatest commandment. And the second is like it: "Love your neighbor as yourself." All the Law and the Prophets hang on these two commandments (Matt. 22:37-40).

Jesus clearly said this "spill-over" into our relationships with others in this "one new humanity"—the Church—would profoundly affect the world around us:

> I have given them the glory that you gave me, that they may be one as we are one: I in them and you in me. May they be brought to complete unity to let the world know that you sent me and have loved them even as you have loved me (John 17:22,23).

God truly is the center of things, in our experience as well as in our theology. When our relationship with him is not right, all of life is impacted. When this relationship is restored, the potential for life as God intended is restored. We have called this *shalom*. Our living relationship with God births emotional and physical health for us, as well as healthy, fulfilling relationships with others and with the creation itself. As we experience this restoration, we are "being transformed into his likeness with ever-increasing glory, which comes from the Lord, who is the Spirit" (2 Cor. 3:18).

Purpose, problem, provision, and people—this is the good news of God's kingdom. This is the integrating gospel that brings transformation. In the next chapter, we will look at how we take hold of this for ourselves. God freely offers, but we have to receive the offer—we have to reach out and take hold of it.

APPLICATION TO LIFE

1. Given the strong connection that Jesus made between the gospel and God's kingdom, explain why the kingdom is almost always left out of our presentations of the gospel?

2. Consider the definition of the gospel of the kingdom in this chapter. For those who are currently Christians, is this the gospel you embraced? If not, what part was missing, or what was different? If you are not yet a follower of Jesus, what do you think of this definition?

3. Do the definitions of justice, mercy and grace make sense to you? What do you think of the idea that justice requires that someone pay the price of your sin—either Jesus or you?

4. Consider that God's clear purpose is wrapped up in "one new humanity"—the Church—carrying out his mission of reconciliation. George Gallup, Jr. states that everyone needs a sense of purpose and a sense of belonging.[6] How have you experienced these in your life?

5

TAKING HOLD OF THE GOOD NEWS

Fight the good fight of the faith. Take hold of the eternal life to which you were called when you made your good confession in the presence of many witnesses ... .
Command those who are rich in this present world not to be arrogant nor to put their hope in wealth, which is so uncertain, but to put their hope in God, who richly provides us with everything for our enjoyment. Command them to do good, to be rich in good deeds, and to be generous and willing to share. In this way they will lay up treasure for themselves as a firm foundation for the coming age, so that they may take hold of the life that is truly life.

1 Timothy 6:12, 17-19

Let's suppose someone—with the bank account to back it up—has written me a million-dollar check. People would think me foolish if I just left it in a desk drawer. They would expect me to take it to the bank, endorse it, and deposit it to my account. Then I could begin to enjoy what that money could provide.

Well, an even more valuable gift *has been* delivered for each of us. According to the verses above, this gift "richly provides us with everything for our enjoyment." When we take hold of this gift, we have "taken hold of the life that is truly life." But in many cases this precious gift is like my hypothetical check—still lying in the desk drawer, waiting for someone to take it to the bank and cash it!

Just over 2000 years ago, God sent Jesus to this earth to deliver the good news of his kingdom. Without question, the value of this good news exceeds all worldly wealth, because it can transform our lives in ways we cannot accomplish ourselves. If we understand transformation as changing our very nature, then we know only the God who created us also can transform us at that level.

So why do so many people leave this tremendous gift in the desk drawer? As we've already noted, many times they've received fragmented gospels that make them feel good for a time, but ultimately leave them feeling empty, because they offer little or no authentic transformation. These people have gained "the form of godliness" but not its transforming power (2 Tim. 3:5).

Other people simply may not know *how* to cash the check. When I receive a check, I must *act* to receive its benefits. I must endorse it and present it to be cashed or deposited to my account, or the million dollars is not available to me.

In the case of the good news of the kingdom, God *has* written the check by restoring his kingdom. According to Jesus, this kingdom has great value:

> The kingdom of heaven is like a merchant looking for fine pearls. When he found one of great value, he went away and sold everything he had and bought it. (Matt. 13:45-46)

But to gain access to those resources, we must take action. Let's look at how we cash the check.

Asking the Right Question

I have decided not to ask people anymore if they are "saved," even though it is a biblically-based question. Far too many people say they are "saved"—meaning at some point they "prayed the sinner's prayer." But many of those people have not experienced obvious transformation.

Today, I simply ask people, "Have you considered and taken hold of the good news that Jesus offers?" If they are interested, I engage them in discussion similar to what I am sharing in this book. I'm not suggesting this is the only way to talk to people about their response to God's good news. I merely want to make sure we are presenting the authentic gospel, in a way that enables people to take hold of it. This will transform and integrate their lives *as well as* secure their future.

HOW, THEN, DO WE TAKE HOLD?

With the previous chapter as our backdrop, we are ready to look at how we "cash" God's "check." We'll examine six biblical words and one phrase, as follows:

The Essentials for Taking Hold

Hear, Believe, Receive

The Evidence of Taking Hold

Repent, Confess, Turn

The Public Witness of Taking Hold

Be Baptized

THE ESSENTIALS FOR TAKING HOLD

Hear

> But how can people call for help if they don't know who to trust? And how can they know who to trust if they haven't heard of the One who can be trusted? And how can they hear if nobody tells them? (Rom. 10:14, *THE MESSAGE*)

The first step in taking hold of the good news is hearing the truth of God's word—the truth that God is our friend, not our enemy; that Jesus loves us and gave himself for us; that we can be set free from our sin, our self-centeredness, and from Satan's hold on us; that we can fulfill our God-given destiny of reigning effectively over the sphere of influence God gives us.

We hear the truth of God's word, accompanied by the convicting voice of the Holy Spirit: "When the Counselor comes, whom I will send to you from the Father, the Spirit of truth who goes out from the Father, he will testify about me" (John 15:26). Many millions of people throughout history have heard God's truth proclaimed—with no effect. Others have heard and responded in faith. What made the difference? The work of the Holy Spirit in response to what God knew to be in their hearts (Acts 15:8).

Hearing the truth in a way that births faith requires the interaction of God's Word and God's Spirit. We cannot focus exclusively on the truth of God's Word, nor can we focus exclusively on God's Spirit. We need the counsel a friend gave me a long time ago:

> The Word without the Spirit, you dry up;
> The Spirit without the Word, you blow up;
> The Word and the Spirit together, you grow up!

Believe

> If you confess with your mouth, "Jesus is Lord," and *believe* in your heart that God raised him from the dead, you will be saved. For it is with your heart that you *believe* and are justified, and it is with your mouth that you confess and are saved. As the Scripture says, "Anyone who *trusts* in him will never be put to shame." (Rom. 10:9-11, NIV, emphasis added)

Perhaps the most widely known verse of Scripture, John 3:16, says simply, "For God so loved the world that he gave his one and only Son, that whoever believes in him shall not perish but have eternal life." This verse and other similar ones, like the one quoted above, tell us that *belief* is the key to salvation. Unfortunately, as we discussed in an earlier chapter, because our culture carries a deep misunderstanding of the word *believe*, the exclusive use of those verses has led to the fragmented "just believe gospel."

In today's world, the most prevalent definition of *believe* is, "to accept as true, genuine, or real."[1] That reduces belief to an intellectual agreement that something is true. But to *believe in* God and to *believe in* Jesus means more than that. This is evident in James 2:19—"You believe that there is one God. Good! Even the demons believe that—and shudder." The demons know God is real, but they will not voluntarily follow him!

Biblically, believing in Jesus means *trusting* him with your life by submitting to his Lordship. The evidence is found in the Romans 10 passage above. The same Greek word, *pisteuō*, appears in this passage three times, and is twice translated as *believe* and once as *trusts*.

Further evidence appears in John's gospel, which notes that many people gathered around Jesus, excited by his miracles. "But Jesus would not *entrust* himself to them, for he knew all men" (John 2:24, emphasis added). The Greek word here is *pisteuō*. And it is translated *entrust*. So we can safely imply that believing in Jesus requires you to *entrust* your life into his hands and follow him in service to God's kingdom. People who think they can do a better job of running their lives than Jesus can—these people will never truly follow him in life. They may understand that he is real and authentic, but believing in Jesus requires a change of allegiance from oneself to Jesus.

I will never forget a powerful illustration given by my Greek professor, the late Gertrude Roten. She pointed out two similar prepositions in Greek, *eis* and *en*, both usually translated into English as *in*. But *eis* typically conveys *into*, while *en* means *in*, as in a place. So when we see some form of "believe in Jesus," the preposition is typically *eis*, rarely another preposition *epi*, meaning "upon," and never *en*.

Therefore, we would literally translate this phrase as "believe *into* Jesus." Our English Bibles do not translate it that way because it sounds awkward, but *into* presents a more accurate picture of the real meaning. Professor Roten gave a graphic image to help us understand the real meaning:

> It's like I'm on the second floor of a burning building and I run to the window and look out. I see Jesus with his arms outstretched towards me and he says, "Jump, and I will catch you." *And I believe into his arms.*[2]

This demonstrates what it really means to believe in Jesus. We trust him enough to jump into his arms, committing our very lives into his care. This requires us to rest from our own efforts to save ourselves, trusting the work of Jesus on the cross for our salvation. We simply receive God's gracious offer by faith. And that brings us to the next word.

Receive

> He was in the world, and though the world was made through him, the world did not recognize him. He came to that which was his own, but his own did not *receive* him. Yet to all who *received* him, to those who believed in his name, he gave the right to become children of God—children born not of natural descent, nor of human decision or a husband's will, but born of God. (John 1:10-13, emphasis added)

> I *(Jesus)* will rescue you from your own people and from the Gentiles. I am sending you to them to open their eyes and turn them from darkness to light, and from the power of Satan to God, so that they may *receive forgiveness of sins* and a place among those who are sanctified by faith in me. (Acts 26:17,18, emphasis added)

> Repent and be baptized, every one of you, in the name of Jesus Christ for the forgiveness of your sins. *And you*

> *will receive the gift of the Holy Spirit.* The promise is for you and your children and for all who are far off—for all whom the Lord our God will call. (Acts 2:38,39, emphasis added)

The verb translated as *receive* in these passages is an active word, *lambanō*, rather than a passive one. It means "to reach out and take hold of, to welcome with open arms." In other words, God's gifts are freely given, but we can choose how we receive them.

As we can see in the passages above, when we put our trust in Jesus, we receive three things. First, we receive forgiveness for our sins. The weight of shame and guilt is removed, and we experience new freedom in Jesus. Second, we receive Jesus into our lives as Lord and Savior. We welcome him with open arms, inviting him to take charge of our lives. Third, we receive the Holy Spirit to empower us, guide us into truth, and endow us with spiritual gifts needed to fulfill our service to God's kingdom—to reign effectively with Christ in that part of the kingdom delegated to us.

Hear, believe, and receive. It really is that simple. But how do we know we have *really* trusted God, and not just prayed a prayer that someone suggested? Praying a prayer does not necessarily mean someone has truly trusted in Jesus. As I was considering some of these thoughts several years ago, I sensed the Spirit saying, "Some people think they have prayed a prayer of faith when they haven't. They have just repeated a mantra." A mantra is a verbal spell or mystical formula intended to produce something good. That's belief in magic, not faith in God.

The Bible is very clear. To receive Jesus as Lord and Savior means a change in lifestyle. The change is empowered by the Holy Spirit, not by one's own self-effort. Yet, if no change becomes apparent, then the person likely is living in deception rather than salvation.

So how do we know we have taken hold of the authentic gospel that integrates and transforms life, and we have not just been deceived? Again, we find three key words in Scripture that indicate an authentic transformation.

THE EVIDENCE OF TAKING HOLD

Repent – We Change What We Think

> From that time on Jesus began to preach, "Repent, for the kingdom of heaven has come near." (Matt. 4:17)

We often reduce repentance to a sorrowful feeling about our sins—or at least about being "caught" sinning. An element of sorrow *is* attached to repentance, but it is a different kind of sorrow: "Godly sorrow brings repentance that leads to salvation and leaves no regret, but worldly sorrow brings death" (2 Cor. 7:10). Godly sorrow comes when the Holy Spirit shows that we have sinned against God. Repentance is not the sorrow itself; it is our response to the sorrow.

The New Testament word for repentance is *metanoia*, meaning "a change of mind." True transformation begins with a change of mind. Paul recognized this and pleaded with the Romans to "be transformed by the renewing of your mind" (Rom. 12:2). Eugene Peterson has paraphrased this passage in *The Message*. I love his wording so much, it has become the theme verse of our ministry:

> Don't become so well-adjusted to your culture that you fit into it without even thinking. Instead, fix your attention on God. You'll be changed from the inside out. Readily recognize what he wants from you, and quickly respond to it. Unlike the culture around you, always dragging you down to its level of immaturity, God brings the best out of you, develops well-formed maturity in you.

Too often we do exactly what Paul admonished the Romans *not* to do! We become so well-adjusted to our culture—whether modern or postmodern—we fit into it without even thinking. Unfortunately, *musing*—thinking deeply—isn't popular these days. It is much more popular to *a·muse* ourselves—to avoid thinking. Sadly, people who refuse to think will sooner or later end up deceived.

But as we fix our attention on God, we *will* be "changed from the inside out." Our thinking will change, becoming God-centered rather than human-centered. As this happens, we will begin to change what we say and do.

Confess – We Change What We Say

> Therefore God exalted him to the highest place and gave him the name that is above every name, that at the name of Jesus every knee should bow, in heaven and on earth and under the earth, and every tongue *confess that Jesus Christ is Lord,* to the glory of God the Father. (Phil. 2:9-11, NIV, emphasis added)

> If we claim to be without sin, we deceive ourselves and the truth is not in us. If we *confess our sins,* he is faithful and just and will forgive us our sins and purify us from all unrighteousness. (1 John 1:8,9, emphasis added)

As our minds are changed and renewed, our speech follows. The word for "confess" is *homologeō*, meaning literally *same word.* To confess something is simply to agree with whatever God says about it. God says, "Jesus is Lord," so we say, "Jesus is Lord." This is the "good confession." Paul wrote about this to Timothy as he admonished him, "Fight the good fight of the faith. Take hold of the eternal life to which you were called when you made your good confession in the presence of many witnesses" (1 Tim. 6:12).

Confession is the opposite of denial. When we violate God's command in attitude or action, we are called by Scripture to "confess our sin." That is, we agree with God that we have violated his will and his word. Too often, under the influence of our culture, we say, "That's just the way I am, because of how my parents treated me when I was a child." That is an excuse or denial—or both—but it is *not* confession.

Because neither modernism nor postmodernism recognizes God's revealed truth, our culture doesn't understand sin as "missing the mark." That seems to eliminate the need to confess sin. We may admit something as a mistake or an error in judgment, but rarely do we hear people admitting anymore, "What I did was a sin. I confess this and I repent of it."

We tend to believe that we deal with sin by asking God to forgive. Biblically, however, we deal with sin through confession and repentance. We acknowledge it, change our mind about it, and turn and go a different way. As we do this, God forgives us. Many Christians still carry a lifetime's worth of baggage, simply because they have not followed God's instructions:

> Repent! Turn away from all your offenses; then sin will not be your downfall. Rid yourselves of all the offenses you have committed, and get a new heart and a new spirit. Why will you die, house of Israel? For I take no pleasure in the death of anyone, declares the Sovereign LORD. Repent and live! (Ezek. 18:30-32)

This brings us to the third evidence that we have taken hold of the authentic gospel of the kingdom and are being transformed by God's power.

Turn – We Change What We Do

> First to those in Damascus, then to those in Jerusalem and in all Judea, and to the Gentiles also, I preached that they should repent and turn to God and demonstrate their repentance by their deeds. (Acts 26:20)

As we fix our attention on God, he begins to change the way we think. That births a change in our speaking—we begin to agree with God. And as this happens, God transforms our day-to-day lives, and we begin to see changes in what we are doing.

When we see these three things happening in us or in others, we can rest assured that God is at work. Only he can do this at a heart level. On the surface, people can become religious and conform to a specific set of rules for a time. But what is inside will come out, sooner or later.

When teachers of the law accused Jesus and his disciples of eating with "unclean" hands, he replied:

> What comes out of a man is what makes him 'unclean.' For from within, out of men's hearts, come evil thoughts, sexual immorality, theft, murder, adultery, greed, malice, deceit, lewdness, envy, slander, arrogance and folly. All these evils come from inside and make a man 'unclean'. (Mark 7:20-23)

Thus, New Testament repentance is a change of mind that results in a two-fold change in direction, toward God and away from sin. Paul's words at the beginning of this section clearly support this definition. Someone proclaims the truth of God's word. We hear it, and faith rises in our spirits. We believe and receive God's offer. We repent, as our thoughts begin to reflect God's thoughts. As we pursue relationship with God, we begin to confess, agreeing with what God says. And we begin to change what we do.

We become integrated people, as what we think, say, and do start aligning with each other. This is a life of integrity, defined by Webster's as "the quality or state of being complete or undivided: material, spiritual, or aesthetic wholeness: organic unity."[3]

THE PUBLIC WITNESS OF TAKING HOLD

Be Baptized

> Then Jesus came to them and said, "All authority in heaven and on earth has been given to me. Therefore go and make disciples of all nations, baptizing them in the

> name of the Father and of the Son and of the Holy Spirit, and teaching them to obey everything I have commanded you. And surely I am with you always, to the very end of the age." (Matt. 28:18-20)
>
> Peter replied, "Repent and be baptized, every one of you, in the name of Jesus Christ .... (Acts 2:38)
>
> For we were all baptized by one Spirit into one body—whether Jews or Greeks, slave or free—and we were all given the one Spirit to drink. (1 Cor. 12:13)

Just before Jesus returned to heaven, he told his disciples to go and make disciples of all nations and to baptize them. On the day of Pentecost, when the Church was birthed, the people who heard the apostles' message were convicted of sin and said, "What should we do?" Peter's response was, "Repent and be baptized, every one of you ... ."

Being baptized doesn't save or transform anyone. That is accomplished through our trust in Jesus. Still, Jesus instructed his disciples to baptize those who would follow.

Baptism is a public witness that a person has been born again into God's kingdom. It is a public way of saying, "I have answered Jesus' invitation to follow him. I have died to my old self with him, have been buried with him, and have been raised to new life with him! I am now free to reign with him in his kingdom, ordering my life and my sphere of influence after the principles of that kingdom."

Another aspect of baptism often gets overlooked. When we are born again by God's Spirit, Paul writes that we are "all baptized by one Spirit into one body." As we have already seen, the literal meaning of *baptize* is *immerse*. Thus, we can see that the Holy Spirit immerses us into the church, the body of Christ, the family of God. We do not lose our individuality, but we are no longer alone. We join a community of faith, committed to Christ and to each other. We will look more closely at this in a later chapter.

A Moment of Truth

We have now presented the "big picture" of God's kingdom. We have defined the good news of the kingdom and of the Lord Jesus that the early church proclaimed, and we have noted the fragmented gospels that abound today. And we have looked at how we take hold of this good news.

Now where do you stand regarding all we have discussed?

- **HEAR** – Have you heard the truth of God's Word about the good news of the kingdom of God and the Lord Jesus? Have you also heard the convicting voice of the Holy Spirit saying, "Yes!" to this truth and birthing faith within you?

- **BELIEVE** – Have you "believed into Jesus," trusting your life into his hands, submitting your kingdom to his, so that your life and your sphere of influence become a "province" of God's kingdom? Have you pledged a change of allegiance from self to Jesus as Lord of your life, committing to living as he would, if he were in your shoes?

- **RECEIVE** – Have you received forgiveness for your sins and been "born of the Spirit" as you trusted Jesus as your Savior? Have you trusted Jesus as the one who sends the Holy Spirit? Have you welcomed the Holy Spirit into every part of your life? Have you received his gifts to equip you for effective service in God's kingdom?

- **REPENT** – Are you experiencing a "change of mind?" Are you beginning to think differently, like God thinks, according to his word? Are you finding your thoughts fixed on God, rather than being "so well-adjusted to your culture that you fit into it without even thinking?"

- **CONFESS** – Is your speech changing? Are you saying what God says—that Jesus is Lord, and sin is sin? Are you finding your way out of denial and speaking truth?

- **TURN** – Has there been a turning in your behavior? Is your daily life changing? Is your change of mind and your change of speech becoming visible in your behavior? Have you and others around you begun to note this change with excitement and thanksgiving?

- **BE BAPTIZED** – Have you been baptized, confirming your commitment to Jesus and his kingdom? Have you been immersed into the church as a part of the family of God, the body of Christ committed to carrying out his mission upon this earth?

When we can honestly answer *Yes!* to these questions, then the evidence says we have taken hold of the good news of the kingdom and the Lord Jesus. It also means we "are being transformed into his likeness with ever-increasing glory, which comes from the Lord, who is the Spirit" (2 Cor. 3:18). You could say, "Jesus is now the center of your life." In the next chapter, we will look at how God works in our lives, so that we live from that center.

APPLICATION TO LIFE

1. Matthew records Jesus saying, "The kingdom of heaven is like a merchant looking for fine pearls. When he found one of great value, he went away and sold everything he had and bought it" (13:45,46). What things keep people from taking hold of God's kingdom?

2. What do you think of the idea that "to receive Jesus as Lord and Savior means a change in lifestyle…if no change becomes apparent, then the person is likely living in deception rather than salvation."

3. Christians have argued often about the practice of baptism, about how and when it should be done, and if it is important or not. How important do you believe baptism is? Why?

6

LIVING FROM THE CENTER

The Spirit gives life; the flesh counts for nothing. The words I have spoken to you—they are full of the Spirit and life.

John 6:63

For the Lamb at the center before the throne will be their shepherd; he will lead them to springs of living water. And God will wipe away every tear from their eyes.

Rev. 7:17

Forty years ago on our wedding day, my wife carried a bouquet of her favorite flowers—daisies. Maybe that's why I like this cover, designed by my friend Harriet Miller. But I also like that it succinctly tells the story of the book—integrated life flows from a well-defined center.

Most people looking at this cover immediately will notice the three flowers. A daisy is a cluster of individual petals attached to a very prominent center. As long as the flower is attached to its roots, it lives. If the stem is cut or the petals become detached from the center, they lose their source of life. They soon wither.

This illustrates our human condition. As we have seen, our Creator God intended for us to live in relationship with him. But we decided we could do our own thing instead of hearing and obeying him. Thus we were cut off from the source of authentic, integrated life. In that process, our lives disintegrated into isolated, broken fragments—like the isolated daisy petals lying around on the cover.

In previous chapters, we saw how the good news of the kingdom offers to reverse this curse of death and reopen the way to life. We also looked at how we take hold of this good news. Now we want to examine how this life flow happens. How does Jesus become the center of our lives, releasing new life within us, and transforming our lives by reintegrating them?

Lets look at four commands from Jesus. Jesus does not give commands just to prove he is the boss. As the author of life, he knows how life works, and how we can experience the life flow that keeps things alive and integrated. His commands simply reflect the way to life.

"Come, Follow Me."

One day as Jesus walked on the shore of the Sea of Galilee, he encountered two fishermen, Simon Peter and his brother Andrew. As they were casting their nets into the lake, he called out, "Come, follow me, and I will send you out to fish for people." Their response was immediate: "At once they left their nets and followed him" (Mark. 1:19,20).

A little farther down the shore he encountered another set of brothers, James and John, along with their father, Zebedee. Jesus issued the same call, and this time James and John left *both* their boat *and* their father and followed Jesus.

As he came upon Matthew sitting at the tax collector's booth, he simply said, "Follow me," and Matthew got up and followed him (Matt. 9:9). The same call came to Philip in John 1:43. It's a simple call, and sometimes we get the impression from the responses of Peter, Andrew, James, John, Matthew, Philip and others that it is a simple response.

But clearly, Jesus' invitation required a significant choice to leave behind anything that would get in the way of following. Not everyone was ready to do it. When Jesus came to a young man of great wealth, he said, "If you want to be perfect, go, sell your possessions and give to the poor, and you will have treasure in heaven. Then come, follow me" (Matt. 19:21). This young man's response was different: "He went away sad, because he had great wealth" (Matt. 19:22).

Jesus indicated that *anyone* choosing to follow him would need to leave something behind:

> "Whoever wants to be my disciple must deny themselves and take up their cross and follow me. For whoever wants to save their life will lose it, but whoever loses their life for me will find it. What good will it be for you to gain the whole world, yet forfeit your soul? Or what can you give in exchange for your soul? (Matt. 16:24-26).

Jesus' call to "Follow me" was not an extension of a massive ego, seeking gratification by having followers. Rather, he invited people to follow in his footsteps, because they would find the same authentic life that he exemplified—life as God intended. Jesus warned of a thief who comes "only to steal and kill and destroy." But Jesus came to nullify the thief's intent, for he added, "I have come that they may have life, and have it to the full" (John 10:10).

This is why Jesus' call requires us to lay something aside. As we have defined the gospel of the kingdom, we've discovered that our self-centered attitudes and lifestyles are at the heart of our alienation from God. Jesus knows the desires and priorities that could prevent us from experiencing abundant life. Every roadblock to kingdom living is anchored in a single issue—the desire to live independently of God.

For Peter and Andrew, as well as James and John, if fishing had remained their top priority, they never could have followed Jesus to a different kind of fishing. For the rich young man, wealth would always have blocked his pursuit of abundant life—that's why Jesus called him to lay it aside. The wealthy young man was not the only one to leave this encounter sad; Jesus also went away sad, knowing the man was missing his opportunity for life in all its fullness—an integrated and whole life.

This does not mean wealth is always a problem. One of the first books I remember reading was entitled *God Runs My Business*, the story of R. G. LeTourneau (1888-1969). LeTourneau was a great industrialist, inventor and businessman. He was responsible for nearly 300 patents, and the mammoth machines he built represented nearly 70% of the earthmoving equipment used during World War II.

Throughout his adult life, LeTourneau gave away 90% of his wealth and lived on 10%. Jesus would not have called him to lay down his wealth, because it was not an obstacle to his experience of God's kingdom—it was, in fact, a resource that God could use to bless many others.

Before going on, we must ask a very important question: How does Jesus call *us* today? When Jesus lived physically on this earth, He spoke to people personally. But now, while God is present with us by his Holy Spirit, Jesus is not here in bodily form to present the call in that same manner.

The answer is found in Paul's letter to the Romans:

> Scripture reassures us, "No one who trusts God like this—heart and soul—will ever regret it." It's exactly the same no matter what a person's religious background may be: the same God for all of us, acting the same incredibly generous way to everyone who calls out for help. "Everyone who calls, 'Help, God!' gets help."
>
> But how can people call for help if they don't know who to trust? And how can they know who to trust if they haven't heard of the One who can be trusted? And how can they hear if nobody tells them? And how is anyone going to tell them, unless someone is sent to do it … .
>
> The point is, before you trust, you have to listen. But unless Christ's Word is preached, there's nothing to listen to. (Romans 10:11-16, *THE MESSAGE*)

Clearly, Jesus' call comes as we hear Christ's message proclaimed. Usually this comes through persons who share the message with us. But I've heard testimonies of people who simply picked up the Scriptures, started reading, and the Holy Spirit delivered the call directly.

The call of Jesus—who is the same yesterday, today and forever (Heb. 13:8)—has always been "Come, follow me!" He clearly expects respondents to follow him in everyday life, doing what he would do in the same situations. In the process, we will experience life as it was intended—*shalom*. This is why Paul wrote to the Corinthian Christians, "Follow my example, as I follow the example of Christ" (1 Cor. 11:1).

The early church responded to Jesus' call by confessing their faith with a simple statement—"Jesus is Lord!" Their words implied a submission to him, and a commitment to do what he says. When we respond with that same commitment, we open the way for the life flow of God's Spirit to transform our lives, and we begin the process of bringing all things together into an integrated life. This doesn't happen apart from God's help.

"You Must Be Born Again"

Jesus is Lord. It seems simple to say those three little words, yet Paul noted, "No one can say, 'Jesus is Lord,' except by the Holy Spirit." The key to understanding this is to remember who Paul was. Though he wrote in the abstract language of the Greeks, he described himself as "a Hebrew of Hebrews" (Phil 3:5). He thought like a Hebrew, and in the concrete language and culture of the Hebrews, saying "Jesus is Lord" required a person to live it out. Paul understood that no one could really live this out, apart from God's help.

Jesus understood the same thing, as is evident in his conversation with a man named Nicodemus:

> Now there was a man of the Pharisees named Nicodemus, a member of the Jewish ruling council. He came to Jesus at night and said, "Rabbi, we know you are a teacher who has come from God. For no one could perform the miraculous signs you are doing if God were not with him."

> In reply Jesus declared, "I tell you the truth, no one can see the kingdom of God unless he is born again."
>
> "How can a man be born when he is old?" Nicodemus asked. "Surely he cannot enter a second time into his mother's womb to be born!"
>
> Jesus answered, "I tell you the truth, no one can enter the kingdom of God unless he is born of water and the Spirit. Flesh gives birth to flesh, but the Spirit gives birth to spirit. You should not be surprised at my saying, 'You must be born again.' The wind blows wherever it pleases. You hear its sound, but you cannot tell where it comes from or where it is going. So it is with everyone born of the Spirit." (John 3:1-8)

In previous chapters, we discussed the consequences of Adam and Eve's disobedience in the Garden of Eden. Rebellion shattered the intimate, relational connection with God: "Your iniquities have separated you from your God; your sins have hidden his face from you, so that he will not hear" (Isa. 59:2).

Like Adam and Eve, when we live in rebellion against God, we separate ourselves from his empowering life flow. We are incompetent to carry out his charge to rule over the "province" to which we have been assigned. We are like daises after their stems are cut—the life-giving flow has stopped. We can't even manage our own lives.

Every contemporary twelve-step program acknowledges this reality in some way. Significant and meaningful change can begin only when we admit, "Our lives have become unmanageable." While this may be more visibly evident in lives afflicted with drugs and alcohol, it is nevertheless true for everyone—*no one* is able to rule his or her life properly, the way God intended, apart from a living relationship with him. In this story of Nicodemus' encounter with Jesus, we get more insight into this transforming relationship.

Nicodemus acknowledged what was evident to any open-minded person: "We know you are a teacher who has come from

God. For no one could perform the miraculous signs you are doing if God were not with him." The life of God's kingdom, his love and power, were evident in the transforming miracles Jesus worked among the people he met.

Jesus' reply was straight to the point: "I tell you the truth, no one can see the kingdom of God unless he is born again." Our rebellion gave birth to spiritual death, so that God's love and power—his kingdom life—can only be realized by starting over with a new birth. Nicodemus could not understand this. How could someone enter again into his mother's womb and be born again?

Jesus explained that he was talking about a different kind of birth—a spiritual birth. Just as everyone has been "born of water"—meaning a natural, physical birth—now everyone needs to be "born of the Spirit," because only "the Spirit gives birth to spirit." When we quit running from God, turn to him and embrace him by putting our lives in his hands, an amazing thing happens. God's life takes up residence in our spirits, renewing the possibility of our reigning competently with God in the sphere of influence he assigns to us.

Paul's prayer for the Ephesians—and for all of us—was that we would come to this deep understanding:

> I pray also that the eyes of your heart may be enlightened in order that you may know the hope to which he has called you, the riches of his glorious inheritance in his people, and his incomparably great power for us who believe. That power is the same as the mighty strength he exerted when he raised Christ from the dead and seated him at his right hand in the heavenly realms, far above all rule and authority, power and dominion, and every name that can be invoked, not only in the present age but also in the one to come. (Eph. 1:18-21).

When Jesus took our sin upon himself, he wiped our slates clean. He also sent his Spirit to us *and opened the door of his kingdom.* In Paul's words, he qualified us "to share in the inheritance of his people in the kingdom of light. For he has rescued us from the dominion of darkness and brought us into the kingdom of the Son he loves" (Col. 1:12,13). Now, by the Spirit's power, we are free to do what he intended from the beginning—to reign with him. When we truly understand this, the journey of life transformation and integration is well underway!

In addition to God's present power in our lives, this gift of the Spirit also promises that more is coming. Again, in Paul's words to the Ephesian Christians:

> And you also were included in Christ when you heard the word of truth, the gospel of your salvation. When you believed, you were marked in him with a seal, the promised Holy Spirit, who is a deposit guaranteeing our inheritance until the redemption of those who are God's possession—to the praise of his glory. (Eph. 1:13,14)

Those who accept Jesus' invitation to be born anew receive a "deposit" that pledges an inheritance. And because we know God's kingdom is eternal (John 3:16), we eagerly await the fullness of our inheritance in God's endless kingdom.

At this point, then, our question is this: Now that we have the Spirit, does the Spirit have us? That brings us to the next command of Jesus.

"Receive the Holy Spirit"

I grew up in a denominational church where I don't remember hearing phrases like *baptized with the Spirit* or *filled with the Spirit.* Then in 1975, I met a young Nigerian man at my Bible college. He eventually came to live with us and has been one of my closest friends ever since, even after he and his family returned home to Nigeria in 1984. Joseph and Christie have visited us several times since then, and we have been to Nigeria to visit them as well. Joseph introduced me to these phrases.

When I first met Joseph, I thought he was one of those "wild-eyed Pentecostals" I had been warned about! But as I got to know him, I saw something very different. His faith impacted every aspect of his life. Quite frankly, I felt his walk with Jesus put mine to shame, even though I had lived my whole life in the context of Christianity, and Joseph had been raised as a Muslim. He encountered his first Bible and embraced Jesus as Lord when he was 28-years-old. I was hungry for what I saw in Joseph's life, so with his help I began to study these phrases in the Bible. Let me share some of what I discovered.

On the evening of Resurrection Sunday, Jesus' disciples gathered behind locked doors in Jerusalem, afraid of the Jewish leaders who had succeeded in getting Jesus crucified. Jesus suddenly stood in their midst. In this context, we read these words:

> Again Jesus said, "Peace be with you! As the Father has sent me, I am sending you." And with that he breathed on them and said, *"Receive the Holy Spirit!"* (John 20:21,22, emphasis added).

Two things are clear from this: First, just as Father God had sent Jesus out on a mission, so Jesus was now sending his followers. Second, they could not accomplish this task, apart from the Holy Spirit's empowerment.

So what did Jesus mean when he said, "Receive the Holy Spirit"? The Greek word translated here as *receive* is *lambano*. It is an active word meaning *to reach out and take hold of, to welcome.* An intensive form of the same word, *paralambano*, occurs in the first chapter of John where the message is that Jesus came to his own people, the Jews, but they did *not* receive or welcome him (John 1:11).

Jesus already had told his disciples he would send the Holy Spirit (John 14:15-31). Now he was saying, "When I send the Spirit, welcome him!" We noted earlier that, when a person puts their trust in Jesus, the Holy Spirit comes to live in their spirit, bringing them a new source of life. Jesus sends the Holy Spirit; our part is to receive him. Paul indicates in Romans 8:9 that Jesus always does his part:

"If anyone does not have the Spirit of Christ, they do not belong to Christ." But our enthusiastic welcoming of the Holy Spirit does not come automatically.

Let me paint a picture that may clarify this. Suppose it is a Sunday afternoon. I have just gotten comfortable in my recliner, intending to watch the Chicago Bears on TV. I respond to a knock at the door and find a friend with a suitcase. "I need a place to stay," he says.

Suppose I reply, "Well, come on in. The guest room is at the end of the hall. But please don't bother me, as I have my day planned." Would my friend feel welcomed into my home?

But what if I turn off the TV, saying, "Welcome to my home! Please make yourself comfortable. If you need anything, just let me know." That probably would make my friend feel much more accepted.

Several years ago, as these two pictures flashed before me, I sensed the Lord saying, "That's how it is with the Holy Spirit. When you trust me with your life, I send him. How you receive him is up to you."

Remember that, even though Jesus has all authority in heaven and on earth, he doesn't impose it on anyone. The Holy Spirit is the "Spirit of Jesus" (Acts 16:7). He responds exactly the same way that Jesus does. He doesn't push his way into our lives. Yet, when we welcome him, he exercises his authority freely on our behalf.

This is why the Holy Spirit is called the *parakletos*, which is translated as Comforter, Counselor, or Advocate. It simply means *the one called alongside*. The Spirit walks alongside us instead of pulling us from in the front or pushing from behind. He only takes the room we give him.

Now let's return to the phrases *baptized with the Spirit* and *filled with the Spirit*. Sometime during the forty days following that Resurrection evening when Jesus told his disciples to "receive the Holy Spirit," he again instructed them:

> Do not leave Jerusalem, but wait for the gift my Father promised, which you have heard me speak about. For John baptized with water, but in a few days you will be baptized with the Holy Spirit … .
>
> You will receive power when the Holy Spirit comes on you; and you will be my witnesses in Jerusalem, and in all Judea and Samaria, and to the ends of the earth. (Acts 1:4,5,8)

If we take this term *baptized with the Spirit* literally, it simply means to be immersed in the Spirit. Jesus promised that those who follow his instructions would be immersed in the presence of the Holy Spirit in a way that would empower them to be his witnesses throughout the earth.

These were Jesus' last words before he ascended back to heaven. The disciples returned to Jerusalem and waited expectantly for these words to be fulfilled.

As they waited, I expect they may have reflected on an earlier event in Jesus' life, when he also spoke of water and the Spirit. On a trip to Jerusalem for the celebration of the Feast of Tabernacles, he went into the temple courts and began to teach the people.

> On the last and greatest day of the Feast, Jesus stood and said in a loud voice, "If anyone is thirsty, let him come to me and drink. Whoever believes in me, as the Scripture has said, streams of living water will flow from within him." By this he meant the Spirit, whom those who believed in him were later to receive. (John 7:37-39)

While not a direct quote, this clearly referred to Ezekiel's Old Testament prophecy of a new and eternal temple, where God would "live among the Israelites forever" (Ezek. 43:7). Jesus clearly referred to himself as this eternal temple in John 2:18-21:

> Then the Jews demanded of him, "What miraculous sign can you show us to prove your authority to do all this?"

> Jesus answered them, "Destroy this temple, and I will raise it again in three days."
>
> The Jews replied, "It has taken forty-six years to build this temple, and you are going to raise it in three days?" But the temple he had spoken of was his body.

There, during the Feast of Tabernacles, God's Eternal Temple stood in the courts of the temporal one, a structure that soon would be so thoroughly destroyed by the Romans that "they will not leave one stone on another, because you did not recognize the time of God's coming to you" (Luke 19:44). With a loud voice, Jesus invited those who were thirsty to put their trust in him, promising "streams of living water" would flow from within them by the Spirit.

The prophet Ezekiel painted an incredible scene, noting that he saw water trickle from under the eastern gate of this Eternal Temple. Soon that water rose to ankle deep, then knee deep, then waist deep, and finally to a mighty "river that no one could cross" (Ezek. 47:5). But note what happens wherever this water flows:

> This water flows toward the eastern region and goes down into the Arabah, where it enters the Sea. When it empties into the Sea, the water there becomes fresh. Swarms of living creatures will live wherever the river flows. There will be large numbers of fish, because this water flows there and makes the salt water fresh; so where the river flows everything will live. Fishermen will stand along the shore; from En Gedi to En Eglaim there will be places for spreading nets. The fish will be of many kinds—like the fish of the Great Sea. But the swamps and marshes will not become fresh; they will be left for salt. Fruit trees of all kinds will grow on both banks of the river. Their leaves will not wither, nor will their fruit fail. Every month they will bear, because the water from the sanctuary flows to them. Their fruit will serve for food and their leaves for healing. (vs. 8-12)

What a picture of transformation that touches everything in its path! Surely Jesus' followers were anticipating something like this while they waited in response to his instructions. And, later, when Peter spoke about the events that marked the fulfillment of Jesus' words, he said, "The promise is for you and your children and for all who are far off—for all whom the Lord our God will call" (Acts 2:39). That is still true today.

Now let's look at the second of these two terms, *filled with the Spirit.* Scripture clearly indicates a close connection between the two phrases. When Jesus promised the coming encounter, he said, " ... you will be *baptized* with the Holy Spirit." When Luke reported the fulfillment of that promise, he wrote, "All of them were *filled* with the Holy Spirit" (Acts 2:4).

When we think of something being *filled* we imagine pouring something into a cup or other container until it is *full.* Some understand being *filled with the Holy Spirit* in this way. When they have a certain kind of experience with the Holy Spirit, they are then *filled* and remain *Spirit-filled* from that point on.

But it is clear from the New Testament that being *filled with the Holy Spirit* is not a one-time experience. Jesus' disciples first received the fulfillment of his promise as they gathered on the Day of Pentecost:

> When the day of Pentecost came, they were all together in one place. Suddenly a sound like the blowing of a violent wind came from heaven and filled the whole house where they were sitting. They saw what seemed to be tongues of fire that separated and came to rest on each of them. All of them were *filled with the Holy Spirit* and began to speak in other tongues as the Spirit enabled them. (Acts 2:1-4, emphasis added)

Sometime later, they gathered again. Peter and John had just faced their first opposition for proclaiming Jesus. The Sanhedrin, the Jewish Ruling Council, told the disciples to stop preaching in the name of Jesus. After being released, they went back to the other believers and reported what had happened. Together they entered into earnest prayer, asking God for boldness to continue, even in the face of the threats. Again, Luke records the dramatic answer to their prayers: "After they prayed, the place where they were meeting was shaken. And they were all *filled with the Holy Spirit* and spoke the word of God boldly" (Acts 4:31, emphasis added). The same people gathered together—and the outcome was the same; they were all *filled with the Holy Spirit*.

The word used here is the same form of the verb used in Acts 2:4 when they were filled the first time. Accordingly, we must acknowledge that a person can be filled at least twice. It seems clear, however, that God intends for this to be a continuing experience. Paul admonished the Ephesian Christians to "not get drunk on wine, which leads to debauchery. Instead, be filled with the Spirit" (Eph. 5:18). The verb form here conveys continuing action. It would be translated literally as *keep on being filled with the Spirit.* So I've made this distinction: I see the *baptism of the Spirit* as the *initial filling*, when we first receive or welcome the Holy Spirit into our lives. But then we can be refilled repeatedly.

My long-time friend, mentor, and overseer Harold Bauman suggests a different image to help us understand being *filled with the Holy Spirit*, one that may be especially appropriate, given that in both Old Testament Hebrew *(ruach)* and New Testament Greek *(pneuma),* the same word is used for both *wind* and *spirit*:

> The word *filled* suggests a container. Perhaps more appropriate is the picture of sails filled with the wind. When the sails are filled, the boat is empowered to action. When the sails are empty, there is deadness, no action. When fullness comes, things happen which could not otherwise happen.[1]

What can we conclude from all this? First, when the Holy Spirit convicts us of our sin and our need for God, and we submit our kingdom to his, we are *born again* with a new spiritual birth, and the Holy Spirit resides in our human spirit.

Second, we need to actively welcome the Spirit into our lives. God intends for us to continually submit our will to his, so we are carried along by the wind of the Spirit as it "blows wherever it pleases" (John 3:8). He wants us to be immersed in the river of God's presence, allowing it to carry us along toward the ever-increasing manifestation of his kingdom.

Come, wind of the Spirit, and blow upon us! Come, river of God, and carry us along by your power! As this happens, we will find that our lives are becoming increasingly integrated, that the individual pieces are coming together around a new center, Jesus, as the Spirit empowers us to truly make him the Lord of our lives. And this now brings us to Jesus' fourth command.

"Love One Another"

Life for a follower of Jesus is a "one another" life, not a solitary one. When we are born again by the Spirit, we also are born into a new family. Just like we have discovered in our physical families, our relationships impact how we experience life. Jesus said that others would actually recognize who we are, and what we are about, by how we live out these relationships:

> A new command I give you: Love one another. As I have loved you, so you must love one another. By this everyone will know that you are my disciples, if you love one another. (John 13:34,35)

God's life does not just flow from heaven directly to us; it also flows though us to others, and through others to us. In this way, we grow up to become mature followers of Jesus. God's new community provides the context for living our lives from the center. But healthy community is built by healthy individual followers of Jesus, who take personal responsibility to cooperate with God's transforming Spirit and fulfill their part of the process—formation. And that brings us back to the cover!

You will notice that none of the three daisies is perfect! All have some petals missing, scattered about, disconnected from the center. The same thing is true of our lives. Our walk with Jesus is a journey, and none of us has fully arrived yet. Perfection comes only at the end of the journey, either when Jesus returns or we go to be with him.

This is true for two reasons. One, while we have a full revelation in Christ, our grasp of that revelation is only partial. Paul explained, "For now we see only a reflection as in a mirror; then we shall see face to face. Now I know in part; then I shall know fully, even as I am fully known" (1 Cor. 13:12). This requires us to conduct ourselves with a great deal of humility, because no individual has all the answers.

Second, growing up spiritually is like growing up physically. We are born as babies, needing time to develop into responsible adults. It's a journey of learning to live by the Spirit within us, of learning to live with Jesus as the center of our lives. It's to this process of formation that we turn next.

APPLICATION TO LIFE

1. This chapter suggests that when Jesus calls people to "Come, follow me," it always involves leaving something behind. Do you agree? If so, what have you had to leave behind to follow him? What might he be asking you to leave behind now?

2. Explain in your own words what it means to be "born of the Spirit." Why is this so important?

3. How have you welcomed the Holy Spirit into your life in the past? How are you continuing to do that now, so that you can "keep on being filled with the Spirit?"

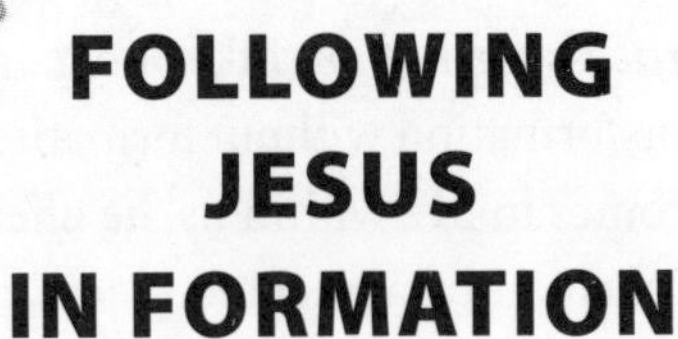

7 FOLLOWING JESUS IN FORMATION

Like newborn babies, crave pure spiritual milk,
so that by it you may grow up in your salvation,
now that you have tasted that the Lord is good.

1 Peter 2:2,3

"We can become like Christ by doing one thing—by following him in the overall style of life he chose for himself. If we have faith in Christ, we must believe that he knew how to live … . Spiritual growth and vitality stem from what we actually do with our lives, from the habits we form, and from the character that results."

Dallas Willard[1]

I played high school basketball, not because I was an athlete, but because my graduating class included only 19 students. Anyone who could dribble the ball and was willing to practice made the team. Like the real athletes, though, I learned the truth of "no gain without pain." I still wince when I remember the laps around the gym, and up and down the stairs. I did all that, so I could put on an Elnora High School uniform and sit on the bench. On rare occasions, I actually got into a game—usually in the closing minutes, when I could not inflict any damage on the outcome!

Paul understood the "no gain without pain" discipline of the athlete as he wrote, "Everyone who competes in the games goes into strict training. They do it to get a crown that will not last; but we do it to get a crown that will last forever" (1 Cor. 9:25). The last part of that statement indicates a similar need for discipline for all who want to mature in their faith and finish well—they "go into strict training."

We call this process *formation.* Like "no gain without pain," we also can say "no transformation without formation." When the Spirit of the Living God comes to live within us, he offers to transform our lives, reclaiming broken and fragmented pieces, and restoring them into a whole, integrated life. But this does not happen automatically. Anything of value to God's kingdom is a joint venture between him and his people. God supplies the ability to change, but we are not passive objects or observers of that change. *Transformation* is the Spirit's work, but *formation* grows from our cooperation.

Finally, we also can say there is "no disciple without discipline." A disciple follows Jesus and learns from him—in that way, he or she is being formed into Jesus' image.

Discipline isn't popular in our world. The word typically carries negative connotations from association with punishment. But the word carries another meaning: *Merriam-Webster's Collegiate Dictionary* lists this definition: "training or experience that corrects, molds, or perfects the mental faculties or moral character."[2]

This brings us to the subject of spiritual disciplines. When we practice spiritual disciplines, we are imitating Jesus and learning from him. And the disciplines help us form new habits to replace our old ones that accompanied us when we entered God's kingdom.

THE POWER OF HABITS

My friend Wally Fahrer introduced me to what he called "The Lazarus Principle." He noted that John 11 includes an account of Jesus' arrival at the home of Lazarus and his sisters, Mary and Martha. Interestingly enough, Jesus came four days after Lazarus died. Jesus told the crowd to take away the stone from the tomb's entrance. Then he called, "Lazarus, come out!" Lazarus walked out with the burial linens still wrapped around him. Jesus then said, "Take off the grave clothes and let him go" (v.44).

Wally's comment was this: "Isn't it interesting that Jesus chose not to unwrap him? The one who could speak life into the midst of death could certainly have unwrapped him, but he didn't. He left that for his friends to do."

We can apply this to our own lives in two ways. First, when we come into new life in God's kingdom, we often come with "grave clothes" from our old lifestyles. Second, we need help from other followers of Jesus to get free. We will address this process in detail in the next chapter. For now, let's learn more about those "grave clothes."

Grave Clothes

Our "grave clothes" come in two forms. First are the lies that Satan succeeds in getting into our minds. Jesus described the devil like this: "When he lies, he speaks his native language, for he is a liar and the father of lies" (John 8:44).

Satan's lies often come through difficult experiences. For example, suppose a parent, teacher, pastor, or other authority figure violates a child in some way. Satan whispers in the mind of the child, "You can't trust anyone in authority."

Then he manages to connect those lies to God, so we believe something false about his character and his intentions. Satan will do everything he can to keep us from putting our trust in God. If he can convince us that God is cruel, distant, and untrustworthy, then we probably won't trust him with our lives.

Satan also lies about us. For example, if we fail at something the devil says, "You will never amount to anything." These lies usually include some kind of accusation. That should not surprise us, given that his very name Satan means "the accuser." He truly is, as John wrote, "the accuser of our brothers and sisters" (Rev. 12:10).

My friend Dennis Chaput has developed a wonderful tool, called *The Redeemer's Key*, to help persons work through the lies we bring with us when we enter God's kingdom. We need to remove those "grave clothes," replacing them with truth from God's Word.[3]

Second, we often enter God's kingdom with unhealthy *habits* formed by sinful lifestyles. Our "grave clothes" can be woven from our own habits, or from other people whose habits and choices impact us. A habit is "a recurrent, often unconscious pattern of behavior that is acquired through frequent repetition; an established disposition of the mind or character; customary manner or practice; an addiction."[4]

Sinful thought patterns and actions are habit-forming in themselves. Repetition increases their hold over us, and as they become more and more embedded within us, we grow less and less conscious of them. We react in unhealthy ways to the guilt and shame we experience from our own sin, and to the hurt we experience from the sins of others. Our negative reactions tend to reinforce our habits, and the whole process becomes cyclical.

C.S. Lewis captured the reality of these "grave clothes" in his book, *The Screwtape Letters*. Lewis presents two characters: *Uncle Screwtape* is the devil, and *Wormwood* is an apprentice demon. At one point, Uncle Screwtape is rebuking Wormwood for allowing his "patient" to become a Christian. But he also describes a force working on their behalf:

> I note with displeasure that your patient has become a Christian...There is no need to despair; hundreds of these adult converts have been reclaimed after a brief sojourn in the Enemy's camp and are now with us. All the *habits* of the patient, both mental and bodily, are still in our favor.[5]

Without question, old habits have reclaimed many who have attempted to walk out a new profession of faith in Christ. And old habits have severely reduced the effectiveness of many others who are still in the church.

How do we overcome old habits? Thomas à Kempis (1380-1471) answered that question many years ago: "Habit overcomes habit"[6] Old habits can only be replaced with new ones. Paul set forth this principle when he wrote, "walk by the Spirit, and you will not gratify the desires of the sinful nature" (Gal. 5:16). As the Holy Spirit empowers us to develop new habits, we will successfully shed our old grave clothes.

How, then, do we "walk by the Spirit?" We follow in the footsteps of Jesus, who was "full of the Holy Spirit" (Luke 4:1). Jesus said, "All who have faith in me will do the works I have been doing, and they will do even greater things than these, because I am going to the Father" (John 14:12). If we are to do the things Jesus did, we must live the lifestyle he lived. Jesus' daily, disciplined life prepared him for times of great ministry. We must follow him in discipline, if we expect to follow him in ministry.

The Spiritual Disciplines

In my very first sermon, I quoted from one of my favorite Christian writers, D. Elton Trueblood. I didn't know one of his former students was in the congregation. After the service he introduced himself and asked, "Would you like to meet Dr. Trueblood sometime?"

"Of course," I replied.

The next week I received a letter from Dr. Trueblood inviting me to come to Richmond, Indiana, where he served as Professor Emeritus at Earlham College. Everyone who learned of my invitation wanted to accompany me!

As an alternative, we invited Dr. Trueblood to spend a day at our church in Indianapolis. He preached in the morning service and then ate lunch with us and spent a good part of the afternoon sharing. It was one of the most memorable times of my life.

Sometime later I had lunch with one of my Bible college professors. I shared some things I learned from Dr. Trueblood concerning spiritual disciplines. To my great surprise and dismay, he laughed and said, "Why do you talk about discipline; don't you understand this is the age of grace?"

To set discipline and grace in opposition to each other is to totally misunderstand both. This view confuses God's grace with what Dietrich Bonhoeffer called "cheap grace."[7] This false notion sees grace as *permission to stay the same*, when in reality, it is *God's powerful tool to change us into his image.* Discipline is not a mere expression of legalism and bondage. It is the doorway to freedom. No athlete will ever be free to perform in the Olympics without the consistent practice of discipline. No Christian will ever be free to reign effectively with Christ, without following him in the spiritual disciplines he practiced.

Spiritual disciplines are activities that "bring us into more effective cooperation with Christ and his kingdom...to make us capable of receiving more of his life and power without harm to ourselves or others."[8] They are vital steps toward integrating the physical and spiritual parts of our lives, reflecting the transformation Jesus promised to those who would follow him. Dallas Willard expresses it this way:

> *Whatever is purely mental cannot transform the self....* One of the greatest deceptions in the practice of the Christian religion is the idea that all that really matters is our internal feelings, ideas, beliefs, and intentions. It is this mistake about the psychology of the human being that more than anything else divorces salvation from life, leaving us a headful of vital truths about God and a body unable to fend off sin.[9]

This book can only offer a brief introduction to the spiritual disciplines. If this introduction whets your appetite for more, I recommend *The Spirit of the Disciplines: Understanding How God Changes Lives*, by Dallas Willard.[10] Willard divides the spiritual disciplines into two categories: disciplines of abstinence and disciplines of engagement.[11] The disciplines of abstinence strengthen us to say "no" to pressures from our old nature, and from the prevailing culture. This makes room for us to say "yes" to the disciplines of engagement, through which we encounter the transforming work of the Holy Spirit.

The person who practices the disciplines of abstinence is heeding the words of Peter: "Dear friends, I urge you, as foreigners and exiles, to abstain from sinful desires, which war against your soul" (1 Pet. 2:11). Paul showed the interaction of disciplines of abstinence and engagement in his admonition to "put off" and "put on":

> You were taught, with regard to your former way of life, to *put off your old self*, which is being corrupted by its deceitful desires; to be made new in the attitude of your minds; and to *put on the new self*, created to be like God in true righteousness and holiness. (Eph. 4:22-24, emphasis added)

We must always emphasize the disciplines of engagement. If we concentrate on abstinence, we end up hard, legalistic, religious people. The full life comes when we recognize the need for abstinence, so we can make room for God's transforming power, released in our lives.

Spiritual disciplines don't require jumping through hoops to become a spiritual giant. They don't enable us to manipulate God into doing what we want. They're not magic. They're simply part of answering the call of Jesus to "Come, follow me!" They help us develop the lifestyle that frees us from our old grave clothes, so we can thrive, following Christ in his kingdom.

THE DISCIPLINES OF ENGAGEMENT

Let's look at some disciplines that Jesus practiced. First, we'll examine the disciplines of engagement, where we want to place our major focus. Then, we'll look at some disciplines of abstinence that free us to practice the former.

Worship and Service

A. W. Tozer wrote that Jesus came to this earth "in order that he might make worshipers out of rebels."[12] As usual, Jesus himself set the pattern for our worship.

To worship is simply to ascribe worth, as David did to God: "Ascribe to the LORD, you heavenly beings, ascribe to the LORD glory and strength. Ascribe to the LORD the glory due his name; worship the LORD in the splendor of his holiness" (Ps. 29:1,2). Jesus did this in a myriad of ways, perhaps best summarized in his prayer to Father God in John 17:4, "I have brought you glory on earth by finishing the work you gave me to do." Throughout his life, Jesus respected and honored Father God by seeking him out, listening, and then following what he heard and saw.

Paul captured this essence of worship in Romans 12:1, which is expressed in a delightful way in Eugene Peterson's paraphrase, *The Message*: "So here's what I want you to do, God helping you: Take your everyday, ordinary life—your sleeping, eating, going-to-work, and walking-around life—and place it before God as an offering." I don't mean to deny that we worship God as we sing during a "worship service." Psalm 100 is a classic example of a psalm of praise that Israel used to worship God:

> Shout for joy to the LORD, all the earth.
>
> Worship the LORD with gladness; come before him with joyful songs.
>
> Know that the LORD is God. It is he who made us, and we are his; we are his people, the sheep of his pasture.
>
> Enter his gates with thanksgiving and his courts with praise; give thanks to him and praise his name.
>
> For the LORD is good and his love endures forever; his faithfulness continues through all generations.

I enjoy the privilege of corporate worship as much as anyone else. But I see a problem when we limit our definition of worship to what happens on Sunday morning at church. We miss the comprehensive nature of a lifestyle of worship.

This highlights the connection between worship and service. In response to the devil's temptation for Jesus to worship him, our Lord replied, "Worship the Lord your God and serve him only" (Luke 4:8). And, speaking of himself, he said, "the Son of Man did not come to be served, but to serve, and to give his life as a ransom for many" (Matt. 20:28). Jesus linked his life of serving others with the greatest act of worship the world would ever see—in obedience to the mission the Father assigned him, he allowed himself to be crucified, pouring out his life as a sacrifice for the sins of the whole world.

When we see worship as a comprehensive lifestyle, we'll find service on the other side of the same coin. Fragmentation happens when the two are separated, so that we "worship" God on Sundays and "serve" the gods of our culture—money, pleasure, power, and sex—the rest of the week.

This happened in Old Testament times among a group of people who lived in Samaria after the Israelites were taken into captivity. These people did not know how to worship Yahweh, the God of Israel, in whose land they were now living. Things started going badly for them, so they asked for help.

The king sent one of Israel's priests to teach the people how to worship the one true God. The end result was "They *worshiped* the LORD, but they also *served* their own gods in accordance with the customs of the nations from which they had been brought" (2 Ki. 17:33, emphasis added). The resulting fragmentation was still evident hundreds of years later, as Jesus said to a descendant, "You Samaritans worship what you do not know" (Jn 4:22).

Christians who are unduly influenced by our fragmented culture and its idols suffer a similar disintegration. They *worship* the Lord but *serve* the gods of our culture, just like their non-Christian neighbors. Their faith impacts only their "religious life," not life as a whole, as George Barna has concluded from his research:

> Because the Christian faith is not associated in people's minds with a comprehensively different way of life than they would lead if they were not Christian, the impact of that faith is largely limited to those dimensions of thought and behavior that are obviously religious in nature.[13]

In addressing the Samaritan woman at the well, however, Jesus did not just state the problem: he went on to share good news. He clearly suggested a new day of integrated living, when the spiritual realm would impact this physical world. He said: "Yet a time is coming and has now come when the true worshipers will worship the Father in the Spirit and in truth, for they are the kind of worshipers the Father seeks" (Jn. 4:23). Worship in Spirit births a lifestyle that reflects God's truth in everyday life in this physical world. As we follow Jesus in the disciplines of worship and service, we cultivate his integrated life.

Study and Meditation

In a previous chapter, we saw how God's Spirit resides within those of us who trust Jesus with our lives, immersing us in God's presence. Sometimes we conclude that's all we need. We say, "If I have the Spirit, why do I need to study God's Word?"

A number of years ago, my friend Oscar Marth expressed an answer I'll never forget. He said, "The Word without the Spirit, you dry up. The Spirit without the Word, you blow up. The Spirit and the Word together, you grow up!" I don't know how to say it better than that. You cannot pursue a growing relationship with God without any serious study of his Word. People who pursue that kind of experience become mystics more than disciples, and as Calvin Miller notes, "Mystics without study are only spiritual romantics who want relationship without effort."[14]

Jesus, though full of the Spirit, obviously studied God's written word as well. When faced with the devil's temptations, three times he answered, "It is written..." Then he quoted scriptures that directly addressed each temptation. Like the Psalmist, Jesus understood the value of the word of God in resisting temptation: "I have hidden your word in my heart that I might not sin against you" (Ps. 119:11).

Study and meditation need to be part of our discipline of God's Word. We study to gain knowledge and understanding of God's purposes and desires. As Paul prepared to address the subject of spiritual gifts, he wrote, "I do not want you to be ignorant." Biblical ignorance is *not* bliss, for how can we follow Jesus if we don't know what he did and said?

Knowledge is just the starting point, for Paul reminds us:

> We know that "We all possess knowledge." But knowledge puffs up while love builds up. Those who think they know something do not yet know as they ought to know. But whoever loves God is known by God. (1 Cor. 8:1,2)

In addition to studying God's Word, we need to meditate on it. We need to muse deeply on a portion of Scripture until the God behind that Word, the God who *is* love, gets through to us. This keeps life integrated.

As a seminary student, I discovered both faculty and students generally fell into two groups. For some, the more they learned, the more impressed they were with *what they knew*. For others, the more they learned, the more impressed they were with *what they still had to learn.* Knowledge by itself tends to "puff up." The practice of meditation offsets this tendency, for it opens our ears to hear his Spirit.

Prayer

Jesus was a man of prayer, especially when facing important decisions. The night before he selected the twelve apostles, he "went out to a mountainside to pray, and spent the night praying to God" (Luke 6:12). Facing impending crucifixion, he went to a favorite place, Gethsemane, and poured out his heart to his Father: "If it is possible, may this cup be taken from me. Yet not as I will, but as you will" (Matt. 26:39).

During my first trip to Israel, our tour leader asked me to lead in prayer at Gethsemane. Some people believe the older olive trees in this garden may have been there when Jesus was! In that context, I was overcome to the point that I could not finish my prayer. I realized I was praying at the site where Jesus won victory over sin. He carried it out the next day on Calvary, but Jesus' prayer here in the Garden of Gethsemane really settled the issue—he would submit to the Father's plan.

Too often, people see praying and doing as contrasting activities. I remember a seminary professor recounting a situation that happened the year before I began my studies. Some monks from a local Episcopalian monastery attended a weekly forum to describe their lives of prayer. After they shared, one of the more activist students asked, "How can you spend so much time praying when there is so much to be done?"

"Sir," the monk replied, "What evidence do you have that your doing is accomplishing more than my praying?"

In prayer and meditation, we hear the Spirit's voice telling us what to do. Otherwise, we are in danger of a life of unproductive activity. We can be busy, yet have little impact for the kingdom of God.

Over the years, numerous people have told me, "I can't pray, I don't know how." They have in mind some great oration full of old English words such as "thee" and "thou." Prayer does not need to be in King James English—God understands contemporary language. Prayer is nothing more than simple conversation with God, like you would have with any person today.

Like any good conversation, it includes listening as well as talking. Even in our everyday conversations, most of us are better at talking than listening. A major problem is that the average person says about 125 words per minute. Because we think and process information at speeds of 400-500 words per minute, we can "listen" to someone, and still have another conversation or two running in our minds! Most of us have to cultivate good listening skills and practice them often.

When it comes to conversation with God, the problem is compounded even further. If it's hard to concentrate and listen to a person seated in front of me, it's even harder when the God who is present is also invisible!

Beyond that, many of us learned as children to "say our prayers." We learned to talk to God, listing our requests, and we expected him to do all the listening. I don't know about you, but I don't always enjoy conversations with people who do all the talking. I've wondered if God feels the same way. What if we began our prayers by asking God what is on his mind, instead of telling him what is on ours?

There is nothing wrong with bringing our requests to God, but we also need to cultivate the habit of listening. A friend helped me learn this part of prayer years ago. I lacked confidence in my ability to hear God, even if I tried. How would I know if I was hearing God or just hearing myself?

My friend reminded me of the words of Jesus in John 10. Comparing himself to a shepherd, Jesus explained, " ... his sheep follow him because they know his voice" (v.4). Jesus also said this:

> "Ask and it will be given to you; seek and you will find; knock and the door will be opened to you. For everyone who asks receives; those who seek find; and to those who knock, the door will be opened.
>
> "Which of you, if your son asks for bread, will give him a stone? Or if he asks for a fish, will give him a snake? If you, then, though you are evil, know how to give good gifts to your children, how much more will your Father in heaven give good gifts to those who ask him! (Matt. 7:7-11)

Putting all of this together, I have learned to ask for spiritual bread from heaven—I ask for him to share his thoughts from his throne. Often when I ask, thoughts come to me that I know are beyond me. They are bread from heaven, giving direction for my life.

I have never heard an audible voice, and I am not perfect in knowing what is from God and what is from me. But I have learned I can check Scripture to see if what I think I heard is consistent with God's written Word, as he will not contradict himself. And also, I often ask trusted Christian friends, and I consider their counsel.

Finally, with practice, we can follow Paul's advice, learning to "pray continually" (1 Thess. 5:17). We can cultivate the habit of living in a way that is tuned in to God, expecting a life-giving conversation as we go about our day-to-day lives.

Submission

Submission is another biblical concept, like discipline and authority, that has fallen on hard times in our age of autonomy. We have this thirst for absolute freedom, but we don't realize that absolute freedom usually ends in bondage to oneself. Giving in to every whim or urge that strikes our fancy may sound great, but it often produces more bondage than freedom. Observe any addict!

Jesus understood the discipline of submission as the way to freedom, and he practiced it continually. He would do "only what he sees his Father doing," and would only "speak just what the Father has taught me" (Jn. 5:19; 8:28).

Submission is related to, but not the same as, obedience. You can walk in submission without being obedient. The classic example is found in Acts 4-5. Peter and John were called before the Sanhedrin, Israel's supreme authority, because they were preaching about Jesus. The rulers released the disciples after ordering them to stop proclaiming their good news immediately.

Peter and John went right back to the Temple, teaching people about Jesus. Again, they were called before the Sanhedrin to explain their disobedience. "We must obey God rather than man," they replied.

They were flogged and released—no minor punishment, by the way! They submitted to the flogging and went away "rejoicing because they had been counted worthy of suffering disgrace for the Name" (Acts 5:41). Peter and John respected the authority of the Sanhedrin and submitted to their punishment. Yet they refused to obey, because they had been called to preach by a higher authority, King Jesus.

On the other hand, it is possible to practice obedience without submission. Submission starts as an attitude of the heart. Both children and adults sometimes obey authority under the threat of force, while inside they are seething with anger. This is obedience, but not submission. Once the threat of force is removed, they often demonstrate their lack of submission—and their obedience goes out the window as well.

In the discipline of submission, we submit to the authority that God places over us, both in the civilian world and in the kingdom of God. In fact, it's in learning to submit to these authorities—particularly as children recognize their parents' authority—that we learn to submit to God.

The Apostle John made a connection between the seen and the unseen world when he wrote, " ... if we do not love a fellow believer, whom we have seen, we cannot love God, whom we have not seen." (1 John 4:20). I think the same principle can be applied to submission: Anyone who will not submit to earthly authorities also won't submit to the authority of the unseen God. Many people move from one church to another, because they "answer only to God." They are deceived, for they are rebelling against those who could train them to submit to God's authority.

Of course, authorities in God's kingdom are called to follow Jesus in exercising their authority. Kingdom authorities are servants, not overlords, as we have noted previously. When authorities function this way, and the people they serve practice submission, God's kingdom flourishes. When either party takes their cues from the world rather than the Word, problems arise.

This brings us now to the disciplines of abstinence.

THE DISCIPLINES OF ABSTINENCE

At a prayer seminar, I heard that Martin Luther once said "I have so much to do every day that there is no way I can get it done without spending two hours each morning in prayer." I went home determined to get up earlier in the morning to do the same.

But I soon discovered I could not sustain getting up two hours earlier, unless I also went to bed earlier. And I couldn't get to bed two hours earlier without changing my evening habits as well. I could not just add something to my life—I had to change my habits.

The disciplines of abstinence serve a similar purpose. Just as going to bed earlier would open the door to getting up earlier to pray, so these disciplines open the door for more effective practice of the disciplines of engagement.

Solitude and Silence

The Bible explains, "Very early in the morning, while it was still dark, Jesus got up, left the house and went off to a solitary place, where he prayed" (Mark. 1:35). As we withdraw from busy crowds to be alone with God, we find relief from the clutter and clamor of a society that cannot tolerate quietness.

Why do we find silence so hard? I believe there is a connection between this and the general shallowness of our relationships. As the German theologian Eberhard Arnold has written, "People who love one another can be silent together."[15] While my wife and I have times of great conversation, I find it easier to be silent with Gwen than with anyone else. Sometimes we can sit together for an hour or more without any conversation, yet we are deeply aware of each other's presence. In other relationships that don't share the same depth, often I feel I *must* talk—otherwise, what will people think of me?

As we practice the disciplines of silence and solitude, we open the door for more fruitful prayer and meditation—and for the deepening of our love relationship with God. As Elijah listened for God to speak to him, God's voice came neither in the wind, the fire,

> the amount of social connection people have. Infants and older people die from a lack of relationship, and those in the middle suffer and fail to recover from illness.[17]

Thus *The Integrated Life* became *Integrated Lives*, and one daisy became three! But this raises more questions: Where do we find these relationships that encourage growth and the integration of our lives? What is Christian community? How do we actually live it out? We'll look at these types of questions in the next chapter.

APPLICATION TO LIFE

1. Are you a reader? If not, what is your plan for learning what Jesus did, so you can effectively follow him in life?

2. What place does prayer have in your life? Is it a two-way conversation or do you just talk to God?

3. As you think of following Jesus in these disciplines, what do you think Jesus might be saying to you about your current habits? Where would you like to see change?

FOLLOWING JESUS IN COMMUNITY

Christianity entered history as a new social order, or rather a new social dimension. From the very beginning Christianity was not primarily a "doctrine" but exactly a "community." There was not only a "message" to be proclaimed and delivered, and a "Good News" to be declared. There was precisely a New Community, distinct and peculiar, in the process of growth and formation, to which members were called and recruited. Indeed, "fellowship" was the basic category of Christian existence.

Georges Florovsky[1]

Twelve statues celebrating the "Spirits of America" line the walls of the American Adventure attraction at Disney's Epcot Center. The first one on the left is the "Spirit of Individualism." It celebrates the rugged, pioneering spirit of the men and women who settled this land.

The individualism of the pioneers, though, was different from the individualism of our day. They knew better than to start out on the Oregon Trail alone. They needed each other to survive. Certainly, they took responsibility for their own lives. However, they cultivated an "individualism in community." They knew that community and a healthy sense of individuality were not opposite and competing realities.

Jesus recognized this same principle, for he acknowledged this as the greatest commandment: "'Love the Lord your God with all your heart and with all your soul and with all your strength and with all your mind;' and, 'Love your neighbor as yourself'" (Luke 10:27). The core of the Christian life lies in understanding who we are, in the context of loving relationships with God and with others.

I learned this several years ago while serving as pastor at Tri Lakes Community Church. My overseer and mentor, Keith Yoder, said, "You cannot do your best work for the church if you do not have an identity apart from it." Living in community should not cause a person to lose his or her identity. Healthy individuals make up healthy communities.

Nathaniel Brandon, recognized as the father of the self-esteem movement, also understood that individualism doesn't need to be at odds with healthy community:

> Individuation *(the process of developing healthy personal identity)* raises the specter of isolation to those who have not achieved it and do not understand that far from being the enemy of community, it is its necessary precondition. A healthy society is a union of self-respecting individuals. It is not a coral bush.
>
> A well-realized man or woman is one who has moved successfully along two lines of development that serve and complement each other: the track of individuation and the track of relationship."[2]

The previous chapter addressed the first of Brandon's tracks; this one addresses the second, and it describes how the two fit together.

Today's pervasive individualism is based more on the modern idea of the autonomous self. It gives the idea that a person is accountable to no one, needs no one, and is concerned about no one other than self. It is actually the opposite of the attitude exhibited by our early pioneers.

Instead of concern for the community, it puts self first without regard for others. One result is out-of-control capitalism, where a basketball player receives more than $301,000 *per game*, and corporate executives earn multi-million-dollar bonuses—even if their performance contributed significantly to driving our economy into a ditch. At the same time, millions of others must eke out a living on a minimum wage.

And, instead of taking responsibility for myself, the contemporary mindset makes others responsible for my well being, creating an entitlement mindset. "If I can't have what I want, it's your fault—and it's your responsibility to make it happen for me!" This thinking leads some to conclude that socialism is the answer to the problems that capitalism has created. But if people refuse to take responsibility for themselves, no government on earth has the resources to bail out everyone.

These ideas, coupled with fallen human nature and the church's failure to proclaim the gospel of the kingdom, have produced many contemporary problems. Branden, writing in the last decade of the 20th century, recognized the fallacies of this line of thought:

> The American culture is a battleground between the values of self-responsibility and the values of entitlement. This is not the only cultural conflict we can see around us, but it is the one most relevant to self-esteem. It is also at the root of many of the others.
>
> We are social beings who realize our humanity fully only in the context of community. The values of our community can inspire the best in us or the worst...A culture in which human beings are held accountable for their actions supports self-esteem; a culture in which no one is held accountable for anything breeds demoralization and self-contempt. A culture that prizes self-responsibility fosters self-esteem; a culture in which people are encouraged to see themselves as victims fosters dependency, passivity, and the mentality of entitlement. The evidence for these observations is all around us.[3]

While we live in a perilous time, it is also a time of great opportunity. The time has never been better to rediscover what it means to follow Jesus in healthy Christian community, where people take responsibility for their own lives *and* help each other become all God meant them to be.

Community in the Nature of God

The original community is ancient—actually eternal. It exists within God's very nature. In the Bible's very first chapter, we read, "Then God said, 'Let us make human beings in our image, in our likeness…'" (Gen. 1:26) The Hebrew word for God, *Elohim*, is a plural noun, consistent with the words "let us…"

Years ago, I heard from my favorite seminary professor, J. C. Wenger, "The New is in the Old concealed, the Old is in the New revealed." What is present but concealed in the Old Testament (that God is a plurality) is revealed in the New (that God is Trinity—Father, Son, and Holy Spirit). This is an eternal community.

Jesus spoke clearly on several occasions about the relationship he enjoyed with Father God:

> The Son can do nothing by himself; he can do only what he sees his Father doing, because whatever the Father does the Son also does. For the Father loves the Son and shows him all he does. (John 5:19-20)
>
> I and the Father are one. (John 10:30)

Then in John 14:26, he links all three members of the Trinity: "But the Advocate, the Holy Spirit, whom the Father will send in my name, will teach you all things and will remind you of everything I have said to you."

God's triune nature is hard to comprehend. How can God be three and one at the same time? It has always been a stumbling block to Jews and Muslims, the other major monotheistic religions of the world, who often think Christians have three gods. Thus, while Muslims think of Jesus as the greatest of the prophets, they cannot conceive of him as God.

But if Jesus were the greatest of prophets, then we must hear his words as they are recorded in Scripture. And this can only lead us to conclude that Father God, the Holy Spirit, and Jesus the Son enjoyed an intense fellowship with each other—and set the pattern for our own relationships. As Brian Hathaway expresses it:

> It was to establish relationships like those enjoyed within the trinity that Jesus came to earth. He prayed for it. He died for it. He sent the Holy Spirit for it. He is interceding for it now. He is coming back for it.[4]

Community in the Old Testament

Given God's relational nature, and knowing that humanity was created in God's image, we aren't surprised to read God's declaration, "It is not good for the man to be alone..." (Gen 2:18). We see him creating a companion.

It would be a mistake to think this need for companionship and relationship was limited to the need for a spouse. Later in Genesis, as God called the individual Abraham, the purpose was to create a "great nation" through which "all peoples on earth" would be blessed.

Years later God repeated this call to Abraham's descendants, the children of Israel gathered at Mt. Sinai: "Although the whole earth is mine, you will be for me a kingdom of priests and a holy nation" (Ex. 19:5,6). God has always called out a *people*, not a disconnected collection of individuals.

God treated the Israelites as a people, teaching them a reality I learned from one of my mentors, Dean Hochstetler: "When someone sins, someone suffers." As a community, our actions impact others.

We see this in the case of Achan, an Israelite who ignored God's instruction to take no personal spoils when Israel defeated Jericho. Achan's entire family suffered for his sin, plus 36 men lost their lives in the next battle (Joshua 7).

God also taught the Israelites the importance of helping one another in little groups of two or three:

> Two are better than one, because they have a good return for their labor: If they fall down, they can help each other up. But pity those who fall and have no one to help them up!
>
> Also, if two lie down together, they will keep warm. But how can one keep warm alone?
>
> Though one may be overpowered, two can defend themselves. A cord of three strands is not quickly broken. (Eccles. 4:9-12)

Jesus and Community

As Jesus began his public ministry, large crowds began to gather. He taught and ministered to them, but he never focused on them. These crowds undoubtedly contained both curious onlookers and persons who were serious about following him. He called this latter group his "disciples." When he returned to be with his Father after his resurrection, a total of 120 disciples gathered in Jerusalem (Acts 1:15).

One night Jesus went to a mountainside to pray. Then, "when morning came, he called his disciples to him and chose twelve of them" (Luke 6:13). This small group of disciples, also called apostles, spent the rest of his earthly ministry with him. To them, he taught and ministered on a deeper level. After teaching the larger crowds, "when he was alone with his own disciples, he explained everything" (Mark 4:34). This small group of twelve men formed Christ's new community—the core of the first church.

Scripture also indicates that, within this new community of 12 persons, there was an inner circle of three that included Peter, James, and John. Jesus invested even more time with these three, as a smaller leadership circle. Accordingly, it should be no surprise to hear Peter and John mentioned more than the others in the church's early days, especially prior to Paul's conversion.

Jesus instructed his followers, "A new command I give you: Love one another. As I have loved you, so you must love one another. By this everyone will know that you are my disciples, if you love one another" (John 13:34-35). In other words, his church would be known primarily for their caring relationships.

This supports Florovsky's words at the beginning of this chapter, "From the very beginning Christianity was not primarily a 'doctrine' but exactly a 'community.'" If we can recover this understanding of Christianity, we have great opportunity to influence our fragmented and frayed world.

Community in the New Testament Church

To describe New Testament Christian community, we need to examine two words. The first is *ekklesia,* the Greek word usually translated *church*. It means literally, the "called out ones, an assembly." This word was a political term, not a religious one. It commonly referred to those called out or assembled in the public affairs of a free state.

New Testament writers could have chosen the common word for a religious assembly, *panegyris*, but they did not. Their use of *ekklesia* reinforces that they were a people called out to a *kingdom*, not just to a religious society. They were called out to deal with the real, everyday issues of living as citizens of God's kingdom, even while they lived as citizens of a kingdom of this world.

They were called out of a broken and fragmented way of life. And if you are called *out* of something, you are also called *into* something. This brings us to the second word, *koinonia*. This is the actual New Testament word for *community*, usually translated as *fellowship*. It is based on a verb meaning *to share in* and means *participation, communion*. Because we *participate* together in the life of Christ (1 Cor. 10:16), we also *share* a special relationship or communion with each other. Peter used some of the same words we saw in Exodus 19 to describe this new *called out* and *called together* people, who shared this unique life:

> But you are a chosen people, a royal priesthood, a holy nation, God's special possession, that you may declare the praises of him who called you out of darkness into his wonderful light. Once you were not a people, but now you are the people of God; once you had not received mercy, but now you have received mercy. (1 Pet. 2:9-10)

The late jazz musician, Duke Ellington, was once asked to define rhythm. He paused, then said, "If you got it, you don't need no definition. And if you don't have it, ain't no definition gonna help!" Christian community is a bit like that: If you have experienced it, you don't ever want to be without it. And if you haven't experienced it, any attempt to define it falls short—but let's attempt it anyway.

Church or Churches?

The *ekklesia*—the church—included all who answered Jesus' call to "Come! Follow me." So is there "one holy Catholic and apostolic Church," as the Nicene Creed states, or are there "churches?" The New Testament uses both singular and plural forms. When speaking of a local church in a given area, Scripture always uses singular: the church in Antioch (Acts 11:19), Jerusalem (Acts 11:22), Ephesus (Acts 20:17), Cenchreae (Rom. 16:1), Corinth (1 Cor. 1:2), at Aquila and Priscilla's house (Rom. 16:5), etc. When speaking of a region, Scripture almost always uses plural: the churches in Syria and Cilicia (Acts 15:41), the Galatian churches (1 Cor. 16:1), the Macedonian churches (2 Cor. 8:1), and "the seven churches in the province of Asia" (Rev. 1:4).

We may conclude that *church* was primarily a local assembly. This fits with the common usage of the word. An *ekklesia* was an actual assembly of people, called together to do business with one another. The churches were all related to one another in Christ, and they helped each other from time to time. When the churches in Judea faced a severe famine, Paul and his companions helped them with a collection from the church in Antioch and the churches of

Galatia and Macedonia (Acts 11:27,30, 2 Cor. 8). But a *church* was a *local* body.

Community in the Local Church

A church was characterized as a "one-anothering" assembly, where people interacted in intimate ways in everyday life:

> Be *devoted to one another* in love. *Honor one another* above yourselves. (Rom. 12:10)
>
> You, my brothers and sisters, were called to be free. But do not use your freedom to indulge the sinful nature; rather, *serve one another* humbly in love. (Gal. 5:13)
>
> Be completely humble and gentle; be patient, *bearing with one another* in love. (Eph. 4:2)
>
> *Be kind and compassionate to one another*, *forgiving each other*, just as in Christ God forgave you. (Eph. 4:32)
>
> Let the message of Christ dwell among you richly as you *teach and admonish one another* with all wisdom through psalms, hymns and songs from the Spirit, singing to God with gratitude in your hearts. (Col. 3:16)
>
> Therefore *encourage one another* and *build each other up*, just as in fact you are doing. (1 Thess. 5:11)
>
> And let us consider how we may *spur one another on* toward love and good deeds. (Heb. 10:24)
>
> Therefore *confess your sins to each other* and *pray for each other* so that you may be healed. The prayer of a righteous person is powerful and effective. (James 5:16, emphasis added in all above)

These verses describe the lifestyle pursued by Jesus' early followers. No wonder the book of Acts refers to them as those "who belonged to the Way" (9:2). These "one-another" commands describe how they helped each other grow in their competency to reign with Christ, as they journeyed together on "the Way."

Sadly, the relational interactions mentioned in these Scriptures are foreign to many of today's churches. Because these connections seldom occur in a large group, most contemporary churches simply don't provide an environment that encourages this type of community. This is why the New Testament church experienced *koinonia* on three levels—the large group, the small group, and the "two or three."

Three Levels of Local Church Community

We have already seen three levels of community that Jesus experienced when he was physically here on this earth.

- *Large Group* - The 120 gathered in the Upper Room
- *Small Group* - The 12 he called as his apostles
- *Two or Three* - The inner circle of Peter, James, and John

The early church followed this same pattern. The first two groups—large group and small group—are mentioned together, both in Jerusalem and in Paul's ministry:

> Every day they continued to meet together *in the temple courts.* They broke bread *in their homes* and ate together with glad and sincere hearts, praising God and enjoying the favor of all the people. And the Lord added to their number daily those who were being saved. (Acts 2:46,47, emphasis added)

> Day after day, *in the temple courts* and *from house to house,* they never stopped teaching and proclaiming the good news that Jesus is the Christ. (Acts 5:42, emphasis added)

> You know that I *(Paul)* have not hesitated to preach anything that would be helpful to you but have taught you *publicly* and *from house to house.* I have declared to both Jews and Greeks that they must turn to God in repentance and have faith in our Lord Jesus. (Acts 20:20,21, emphasis added)

The small group is mentioned by itself also, as a "church in a house:"

> Give my greetings to the brothers and sisters at Laodicea, and to Nympha and the church in her house. (Col. 4:15)
>
> Aquila and Priscilla greet you warmly in the Lord, and so does the church that meets at their house. (1 Cor. 16:19)

And, just as Jesus had his little group of Peter, James, and John, so Paul always traveled with a group of companions:

> Paul and his companions traveled throughout the region of Phrygia and Galatia, having been kept by the Holy Spirit from preaching the word in the province of Asia. (Acts 16:6)
>
> Then after fourteen years, I went up again to Jerusalem, this time with Barnabas. I took Titus along also. (Gal. 2:1)

We see other settings of "two or three." For example, when Jesus' followers stumbled in their walk, he instructed them to deal with sin issues in this context of a little group of two or three:

> If a brother or sister sins, go and point out the fault, just between the two of you. If they listen to you, you have won them over. But if they will not listen, take one or two others along, so that 'every matter may be established by the testimony of two or three witnesses....' For where two or three come together in my name, there am I with them. (Matt. 18:15,16,20)

Three Levels of Community in Church History

Perhaps the most effective season of disciple-making since the New Testament came during the life of John Wesley (1703-1791). This era, known as 'The Great Awakening," was the beginning of the Methodist movement. Interestingly, Wesley also followed Jesus and the New Testament Church in utilizing these three levels of community. The Methodists were organized into societies, classes, and bands:

- The *Society* included all class meetings in a given area. Some Society meetings were open, but most were for those who were part of a class. The primary function at a Society meeting was teaching or instruction.
- The *Class Meeting* was a mixed group of 10-12 persons at the core of the Methodist system of discipleship. The Class Meeting functioned more like a family, often stayed together for years, and focused more on personal growth than teaching.
- The smallest group, called a *Band*, consisted of either four men or four women who met weekly to deal with real life issues.

Wesley drew up his "Rules of the Band-Societies," which included these words:

> The design of our meeting is, to obey that command of God, "Confess your faults one to another, and pray one for another, that ye may be healed…."

Among the list of questions they might ask each other, five were asked at every meeting of a Band:

- What known sins have you committed since our last meeting?
- What temptations have you met with?
- How were you delivered?

- What have you thought, said, or done, of which you doubt whether it be sin or not?
- Have you nothing you desire to keep secret?[5]

While every Methodist participated in a Class Meeting, the Bands were optional. They never became as popular as the Class Meetings. But they remained Wesley's favorite, and some scholars believe he eventually regretted not making these mandatory as well.

A New Paradigm

This three-level experience of community provides the context for the formation we described in the previous chapter. It provides an environment for applying truth to life, which leads to transformation. Fragmented lives become whole and integrated, and the *ekklesia* of Jesus experiences *koinonia*!

In this 21st century culture, I believe there are at least four components to the process of forming fragmented persons into mature disciples of Jesus:

- **CARING** – Loving each other with the love we have received from God in Christ

  We love because he first loved us. (1 John 4:19)

- **COACHING** – Drawing out of each other our God-given destiny and call within God's purposes

  The purposes of the human heart are deep waters, but those who have insight draw them out. (Prov. 20:5)

- **MENTORING** – Imparting to each other what God and others have imparted to us, as it applies to their situations

  Praise be to the God and Father of our Lord Jesus Christ, the Father of compassion and the God of all comfort, who comforts us in all our troubles, so that we can comfort those in any trouble with the comfort we ourselves receive from God. (2 Cor. 1:3,4)

- TEACHING – Bringing the truth of Scripture to bear on our lives, undergirding the entire process

  From infancy you have known the Holy Scriptures, which are able to make you wise for salvation through faith in Christ Jesus. All Scripture is God-breathed and is useful for teaching, rebuking, correcting and training in righteousness, so that all God's people may be thoroughly equipped for every good work. (2 Tim. 3:15-17)

Now, how do we mesh these four components of formation with the three levels of community? I believe we need a new paradigm of church to see this happen. A paradigm is a pattern or a way of seeing things, like looking through a particular lens. Often our lenses affect what we see, so it can be difficult to interpret things outside your existing paradigm. Yet, significant breakthroughs can happen if we are able to shift our paradigm and see a different set of possibilities. Consider this diagram:

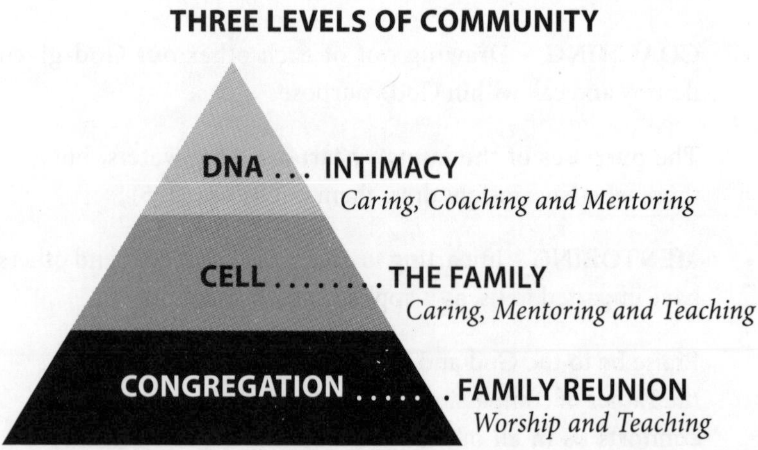

THREE LEVELS OF COMMUNITY

Note the labels suggested for these three levels. First, today's large group, the equivalent of Wesley's societies, we typically call *congregations*. These groups function like family reunions. In this context, the smaller groups within them—the groups that connect in everyday life—also come together regularly to enjoy each other's company, and maybe to learn something, as well.

What can be done effectively in this large group setting? Basically, worship and teaching. I have worshiped in a group as large as almost a million people, when I attended the Promise Keepers men's meeting on the National Mall in Washington, D.C. in 1997. As a person whose primary gifting is teaching, I can teach groups of 20, 200, 2000, even 20,000 or more. In the 18th century, George Whitefield preached to as many as 30,000 people at a time—with no amplification! But it is difficult to do the Scriptural "one-anotherings" in these large groups.

The second level I call a *cell*, because I see it as the church's primary building block. These were Wesley's class meetings. The cell functions like a family—the primary context in which we grow up. What happens here? Families care for one another. Older members mentor and teach younger ones. Parents produce offspring that become new family members. In the same way, these cells are missional groups—they reach out to the broken world and draw others into a relationship with God and with his family. In fact, mission is the center of their lives together, even as it was the center of Jesus' life.

The smallest group I call a *DNA* group. I borrowed this term from Michael Frost and Alan Hirsch. I like it, because it picks up three key functions of this little group—discipleship, nurture, and accountability. I believe it is also where the DNA of God's kingdom gets built into the rhythm of our everyday lives. These were the little groups of four men or four women that Wesley called bands.

This is the place for intimacy, where we deal with life's deepest issues and help each other grow. This is the framework for coaching, mentoring, and caring. This environment provides support, encouragement and accountability, enabling people to make important changes they can't accomplish on their own. How many of us have decided on a lifestyle change, asked God to help us, and then jumped in—only to see it fizzle out within a month? God didn't fail us—but most of us failed to place ourselves in the context he designed to help us.

Transformation and integration happen when truth gets applied to real life, in the context of loving relationships. This is where we live out the "one-another" scriptures, saying to a few close friends, "This is what I want to work on at this point, and I want you to pray for me and hold me accountable." When we nurture that kind of environment, we have prepared a seedbed for the Holy Spirit's work. My friend and coach, Tony Stoltzfus, has developed a number of excellent tools to help us learn how to do this effectively.[6]

I want to stress, though, that accountability is not the same as control. *Accountability* is holding people accountable for the decisions they make. *Control* is trying to make the decision for them. When we do this, we invade their "province" of the kingdom, attempting something that even God will not do.

Over the last 40 years or so, many churches have come to understand the need for small groups. They've tried different models—many of which failed to make much difference in people's lives. As a pastor for 22 years, I know this first-hand. I now believe one key reason is that we failed to understand and implement the smallest of groups—the twos and threes—within the cells. Another reason for failure was a lack of intentionality and focus. It's fun to just hang out with people we enjoy being around—but it doesn't often produce much life change or transformation.

History shows that, when persecution prevents a church from meeting as a large congregation, the church can still thrive if small groups exist. But pity the church that comes under persecution and has only the large group setting! As John Stott has written:

> I do not think it is an exaggeration to say that small groups, Christian family or fellowship groups, are indispensable for our growth into spiritual maturity.[7]

Keeping Community Healthy

Jesus' disciples found that community life is not without its trials. We are all imperfect people, works-in-progress, and whenever we get serious about community and accountability, sooner or later our imperfections will show. This was no less true among the Twelve than among us. James and John came to Jesus with a request: they wanted positions of honor, at Jesus' right and left, when he came into his glory. When the others heard about this, "they became indignant with James and John" (Mark 10:41). They weren't more spiritual than James and John—they just wanted the same seats!

Whenever a new community forms, we can expect it to go through some recognizable phases. The first phase is called "Acquaintance," as people are just getting to know each other. Everyone is happy and excited to be part of the group. Everyone likes everyone else.

But then we get to know each other better, and we find we all have our own little quirks that can be downright annoying to others. Our differing expectations for the group begin to surface. We have entered the second phase of community life, the "Conflict" phase. The temptation at this point is to run. "This group just isn't what I thought it was going to be. I'm going to find another one!" But if we run, what will we do when our next group experience ends up like the first?

My friend Jim Egli refers to these first two phases as "Illusion" and "Disillusion." The rosy picture we have of each other during the acquaintance phase is an illusion, not reality. When this dawns upon us, feelings of disillusionment can rise. But, as Jim says, if we will just press through this phase of disillusion, we can reach the third phase of "Joy," or authentic Christian community.

God is never surprised at our imperfections. That is why he gives clear guidelines in Scripture for dealing with conflict in constructive ways. If we are open and honest with each other, and keep loving each other, we actually have opportunity to glorify God through our conflict! We do this as the Holy Spirit's work becomes evident in the midst of our conflict. We don't avoid real issues, but we remain respectful of each other.

Ken Sande has genuinely blessed the church with his book, *The Peacemaker: A Biblical Guide to Resolving Personal Conflict.*[8] I highly recommend it to every follower of Jesus. It will help us get over the hump of "Disillusion," and on to "Joy!" as we follow Jesus in the discipline of community.

Conclusion

The following quote has been attributed to Richard Halverson, former U.S. Senate Chaplain:

> In the beginning the Church was a fellowship of men and women who centered their lives on the living Christ. They had a personal and vital relationship to the Lord. It transformed them and the world around them. Then the Church moved to Greece, and it became a philosophy. Later it moved to Rome, and it became an institution. Next it moved to Europe and it became a culture. Finally it moved to America, and it became an enterprise. We've got far too many churches and so few fellowships.[9]

May our "enterprise" churches be transformed into the *koinonia* of the *ekklesia*—the community of the called out ones!

Formation to maturity in the context of Christian community prepares us to follow Jesus in his mission—and actually is part of that mission. To this we will turn in our final chapter.

APPLICATION TO LIFE

1. Do you agree that healthy individualism and community are actually complementary, rather than opposites? Why or why not?

2. How have you experienced healthy Christian community? How would you describe it to others?

3. Do you agree that we need to experience community on three levels to grow to maturity? Why or why not?

4. How would you describe the relationship between community and mission?

9

FOLLOWING JESUS IN MISSION

As you sent me into the world,
I have sent them into the world.

Jesus, John 17:18

The Church must send or the church will end.
Mendell Taylor[1]

"God is a sent and sending God." So stated Michael Frost in a video series based on the book he co-authored with Alan Hirsch, *The Shaping of Things to Come*."[2] That is God's very nature—from eternity past to eternity future. This is the actual physical expression of the truth that "God is love" (1 John 4:8). To love is to invest yourself in others. God loved us enough to send himself into our lives.

God Sent Himself into the World

God demonstrated his love for this physical universe when he sent himself to create it:

> In the beginning God created the heavens and the earth. Now the earth was formless and empty, darkness was over the surface of the deep, and the Spirit of God was hovering over the waters… (Gen. 1:1)

God created this earth as a home for his physical creation, especially for humanity as the crown of that creation. It was originally a place of intimate relationship, but our desire to go our own way broke our fellowship with God. So Father God moved on to the next phase of his plan—he sent his Son into this world to redeem and restore it.

The Father Sent the Son

In the Bible's first book, God called to Abraham saying, "Go from your country, your people and your father's household to the land I will show you" (Gen 12:1). The land God showed him became Israel.

Once Abraham's descendants were in this land, God chose one specific city, saying, "Jerusalem, the city where I chose to put my Name" (1 Kings 11:36). The climax of human history would be accomplished in this special place.

Eventually, "when the set time had fully come, God sent his Son" (Gal. 4:4). He was born in Bethlehem, grew up in Nazareth, and lived most of his adult life in the area around the Sea of Galilee. But when it was the right time, he headed to Jerusalem: "As the time approached for him to be taken up to heaven, Jesus resolutely set out for Jerusalem" (Luke 9:51). In this city, God the Son fully demonstrated his love for the human race, sacrificially giving himself on our behalf. And here, he first sent the Spirit to carry on what he had started.

The Son Sent the Spirit

While he was still with his disciples, Jesus told them he would send the Spirit after his departure:

> When the Advocate comes, whom I will send to you from the Father—the Spirit of truth who goes out from the Father—he will testify about me. And you also must testify, for you have been with me from the beginning. (John 15:26,27)

This was fulfilled at the first Pentecost—in Jerusalem—but ten days prior, he gave his final instructions to his followers just before he returned to the Father:

> You will receive power when the Holy Spirit comes on you; and you will be my witnesses in Jerusalem, and in all Judea and Samaria, and to the ends of the earth. (Acts 1:8)

With these words, Jesus *reversed the flow of history*. All prior history moved toward Jerusalem. Now, it would flow the opposite direction, *from* Jerusalem *to* Judea, Samaria, and the ends of the earth!

The Spirit Sends Us

Jesus' first followers were not quick to obey his instructions. After all, Jerusalem was the place where life had been turned upside down, where they had witnessed Jesus' death and resurrection, and where they had their first awesome encounter with the Holy Spirit. Naturally, they would want to stay right there—it was their comfort zone.

But God has his ways to accomplish his purposes: "On that day a great persecution broke out against the church in Jerusalem, and all except the apostles were scattered throughout Judea and Samaria" (Acts 8:1). Note who was scattered—"all except the apostles." While the leaders stayed at the center—at least for the time—*all* the others were sent out to fulfill the instructions Jesus had left with them.

While all were sent out, the church joined with the Holy Spirit in giving explicit instructions for some:

> While they were worshiping the Lord and fasting, the Holy Spirit said, "Set apart for me Barnabas and Saul for the work to which I have called them." So after they had fasted and prayed, they placed their hands on them and sent them off. (Acts 13:2,3)

The early church was an "apostolic" church, meaning "sent out on a mission." This was central to their identity. And they were not sent out as lone rangers—they were part of a koinonia, a fellowship. They were in this mission together. But unfortunately, this apostolic paradigm would change.

THREE PARADIGMS OF CHURCH

In his book, *Churchquake*, C. Peter Wagner writes that the church has known only three basic paradigms throughout its history.

- The Apostolic Paradigm – 1st through 3rd centuries
- The Christendom Paradigm – 4th through Mid-20th century
- The New Apostolic Paradigm – Mid-20th through 21st centuries[3]

Apostolic Paradigm

Throughout the first three centuries, Jesus' church maintained an apostolic mandate. His followers understood *all* were sent out to impact the world with the good news of Jesus and God's kingdom—beginning where they were and spreading to the ends of the earth. They often paid dearly for their allegiance to Jesus. Caesar's soldiers would command Christians to say, "Caesar is Lord!" But they refused, knowing that Jesus had said, "No one can serve two masters" (Matt. 6:24). Many literally lost their heads, simply because they refused to acknowledge Caesar as the supreme Lord of the universe.

But as Tertullian, an early church leader wrote, "The blood of the martyrs is the seed of the church." The harder Rome tried to stamp out the church, the more it spread. Eventually, in 313 AD, the Emperor Constantine issued the Edict of Milan, and Christianity was officially tolerated. By 380 AD, the Emperor Theodosius made

Christianity the official religion of the Roman Empire, birthing the Christendom paradigm of church.

Christendom Paradigm

Many things changed as the church shifted from being persecuted to being the Empire's official religion. Loren Mead, founder and president of The Alban Institute, points out the most significant change was the church's understanding of mission.[4]

In the apostolic paradigm, the edge of each local church was its mission frontier, and every member participated. In Christendom, the church identified with the Empire, and the mission frontier was the edge of the Empire. The political frontier became the mission frontier.

Just as the Empire sent professional soldiers to take care of the Empire's political expansion, so the church began sending professional missionaries to take care of its religious expansion. The vast majority of Christians settled into church life, and their role in mission was simply to support the missionaries from afar.

The influence of the Christendom paradigm held a firm grip on the church for more than 1600 years. Maybe that is why virtually all of our English versions of the Bible translate "the Great Commission" in a very similar way:

> Then Jesus came to them and said, "All authority in heaven and on earth has been given to me. Therefore *go* and *make disciples* of all nations, baptizing them in the name of the Father and of the Son and of the Holy Spirit, and teaching them to obey everything I have commanded you. And surely I am with you always, to the very end of the age." (Matt. 28:18-20, emphasis added)

The primary verb of the second sentence is the imperative, *make disciples*. What is translated as *go* is a participle that would more accurately be translated *having gone* or *as you are going*. In other words, as you are going about your daily life, make disciples!

This does not negate the fact that the Spirit commissioned some, like Barnabas and Paul, for special assignments. But it reinforces that all Christians were involved in the mission of seeing God's kingdom come on this earth—as Jesus had taught them to pray—and to see more people benefiting from an integrated life.

New Apostolic Paradigm

Both Wagner and Mead understand that God is establishing a new paradigm to replace Christendom in our day. Wagner calls it the "New Apostolic" paradigm. Mead states essentially the same thing in different terms—that restoring the apostolic mission will be the center of the new paradigm.

This paradigm shift requires the church to recover the directional change that Jesus pointed to. We have been stuck in an old mindset. Mennonite missiologist Wilbert Shenk put it this way:

> We still have an Old Testament mindset: The Old Testament said, "Come up to Jerusalem." The New Testament says, "Go into all the world." We have it backwards.[5]

Alan Hirsch and Michael Frost speak of this as the church becoming *incarnational* rather than *attractional* in our thinking. We will stop sitting in our church buildings and saying "Come grow with us!" We will find new ways to get outside the church walls and get involved in people's lives in the marketplace—as Jesus did.

We also will recover the integrating gospel of Jesus and God's kingdom. These changes will not come easily, but if we stay with it, we will see a new day in the church. As Loren Mead states:

> We are at the front edges of the greatest transformation of the church that has occurred for 1,600 years. It is by far the

> greatest change that the church has ever experienced in America; it may eventually make the transformation of the Reformation look like a ripple in a pond.
>
> That transformation is occurring because of the persistent call of God that our whole world be made new, and that the church's mission in that world be itself transformed in new patterns of reconciling the world to God.
>
> There are enormous tasks and daunting challenges for those who intend to follow that call, but then the Lord never said it would be easy.[6]

So how will this new understanding of the gospel and of our place on the mission frontier shape a new paradigm of church? How will we go about our mission of sharing the good news of Jesus and of God's kingdom?

THE MINISTRY AND MESSAGE OF RECONCILIATION

Paul's summary of God's intention for this world, and how we fit into his plan, is found in 2 Corinthians 5:17-21:

> Therefore, if anyone is in Christ, the new creation has come: The old has gone, the new is here! All this is from God, who reconciled us to himself through Christ and gave us the ministry of reconciliation: that God was reconciling the world to himself in Christ, not counting people's sins against them. And he has committed to us the message of reconciliation. We are therefore Christ's ambassadors, as though God were making his appeal through us. We implore you on Christ's behalf: Be reconciled to God. God made him who had no sin to be a sin offering for us, so that in him we might become the righteousness of God.

As we are reconciled to God and to each other, we discover the life God intended from the beginning—"a new creation has come!" In this new creation, all of life comes together around Christ, and in company with others.

God intends for every Christian to pass on God's blessings to others. When we revert to the selfish influence of our old nature, or to the devil's deceit and intimidation, we are tempted to keep the blessings to ourselves. This is particularly true with sharing the good news of the kingdom and the Lord Jesus. The devil will do anything to divert people from sharing this message, because it will bring his defeat.

But this message is the center of our calling as followers of Jesus. As this passage from 1 Corinthians reminds us, "God was reconciling the world to himself in Christ." The Great Divide between God and humanity was overcome in this act of reconciliation carried out in Christ. Now we are Jesus' ambassadors to this broken and fragmented world, given both the *ministry* and the *message* of reconciliation.

The Fallacy of the Gift of Evangelism

In this 1 Corinthians passage, Paul indicates that *all* Christians are Christ's ambassadors, tasked with sharing God's message of reconciliation with the world. Somewhere we have gotten the idea that an elite unit with the "gift of evangelism,"—less than 10% of all Christians, according to C. Peter Wagner[7]—is charged with the task of "sharing the good news." It is true that Paul lists "evangelist" as one of the five ministry gifts Christ left with the church when he returned to heaven (Eph. 4:11). However, the task of these five ministries is given in the next two verses:

> To equip his people for works of service, so that the body of Christ may be built up until we all reach unity in the faith and in the knowledge of the Son of God and become mature, attaining to the whole measure of the fullness of Christ. (Eph. 4:12,13)

Persons called by God to function in these five ministry gifts are not called to pass on God's blessings to the world *for us*. Rather, they are called *to equip all of us* to effectively pass on God's blessing in our "province" of the kingdom, our sphere of influence. As we are equipped to function according to our passions and giftings, we will become effective witnesses and ambassadors of Christ. All of this will be built around *the ministry and message of reconciliation*.

Once when speaking of the devil, Jesus said, "When he lies, he speaks his native language, for he is a liar and the father of lies" (John 8:44). The devil is a master of half-truths. He loves to take a little truth and then twist it, subtract from it, or add to it. But remember, *a half-truth taken in its entirety is a whole lie*. It is *true* that Jesus gave to the church the ministry gift of evangelist. It is *not true* that the ministry and message of reconciliation is now left in the hands of about 10 percent of the church who have "the gift of evangelism," and the other 90 percent are exempt from sharing the good news of the kingdom. Every Christian is called to this.

Now let's look at some different ways of fulfilling this calling. First, we'll examine a current model contributing to the unfruitfulness we see in the church, where many people are "saved," but few are truly transformed. Then, I will suggest a biblical paradigm that I believe can help us be much more fruitful in seeing authentic transformation, as people take hold of the good news of God's kingdom.

The Sales Paradigm

We've noted how the church's dependence on 10% of believers to pass on the gospel has hindered the expansion of God's kingdom. But the methods used by many in this 10% may also be counterproductive.

The most prominent model for sharing the good news in our day can best be described as the sales paradigm. Or perhaps we should say the *old* sales paradigm, because there is a lot of talk today about a *new* sales paradigm, focused on selling *solutions* rather than products or *commodities*.[8] That seems to be more compatible with the paradigm I will propose later.

In the old sales paradigm, the salesperson pushes a product. He or she is trained to go for closure, to make a sale—now! Regardless of whether the potential customer really understands the product, your job is to make a pitch that he can't refuse. It's really about the salesperson's selling ability, rather than the customer's needs.

The old sales paradigm for passing on the good news of the kingdom is similar. A salesperson attempts to sell a product to a potential customer. The product is "salvation," meaning forgiveness for one's sins and a secure spot in heaven when you die. The salesperson is completely convinced of the "customer's" need—which is indeed true. But does the *customer* understand that?

In this paradigm, the "salesperson" pushes for closure—to make the sale. Motivation may be right: this person needs Jesus. And because we focus on the product, "salvation," we want to see the person saved—and now! So we lead in a prayer, often before the person has a clue what it is all about. The "customer" repeats words after us—and then we work to assure him of salvation.

I am convinced that sometimes we actually counter the Holy Spirit, who is saying to the person, "Wait a minute, do you understand what you are doing? I want to enter into a lifelong relationship with you." We press for closure because we wonder, "What if they don't pray the prayer and they go out and get hit by a train tonight?" Well, what if we lead them in saying words they don't understand, and they get hit by a train? Will the words they "prayed" get them into heaven? Friends, if we believe this, then I fear that we see faith more like magic, rather than seeing it as trusting God with our very lives.

The new sales paradigm offers solutions rather than products. That's a step forward as a model for passing on the gospel of the kingdom. At least the focus is on helping the person find a solution to life's problems, for now and for eternity, rather than offering a commodity called "salvation" for the price of a "prayer." But I believe there is still a better paradigm. Perhaps it's time to "repent"—to change our minds, thinking some new thoughts about how people come to faith in Christ and join the journey to integration and wholeness.

Thinking New Thoughts

My friend and co-laborer in the kingdom, Ron Klaus, first pointed out the marriage paradigm for passing on the blessing. It's a good biblical picture, clearly revealed in Scripture. Throughout this book, we have seen that the gospel of the kingdom invites us to live in relationship with Jesus, serving God's kingdom in all of life. Scripture pictures this relationship with Jesus as the most intimate of relationships—marriage.

John the Baptist referred to Jesus as the "bridegroom" and to himself as "the friend who attends the bridegroom" (John 3:29). When Jesus was asked why his disciples did not fast, he replied, "How can the guests of the bridegroom mourn while he is with them? The time will come when the bridegroom will be taken from them; then they will fast" (Matt. 9:15).

Paul gave instructions to husbands and wives by using the analogy of Christ and the church:

> For this reason a man will leave his father and mother and be united to his wife, and the two will become one flesh. This is a profound mystery—but I am talking about Christ and the church. (Eph. 5:31,32)

In The Revelation, John described the church as the bride of Christ:

> I saw the Holy City, the new Jerusalem, coming down out of heaven from God, prepared as a bride beautifully dressed for her husband. And I heard a loud voice from the throne saying, "Look! God's dwelling place is now among the people, and he will dwell with them. They will be his people, and God himself will be with them and be their God. (Rev. 21:2,3)

Clearly, the marriage paradigm is a valid picture, describing the relationship between Christ and his church. If that is true, why not think in these terms as we share the gospel with others? Why not offer an invitation to a life-long, committed relationship rather than a "sales" event?

THE MARRIAGE PARADIGM

More than 30 years ago, Dr. James Engel wrote a book titled *What's Gone Wrong With the Harvest?*[9] In this book, he first presented The Engel Scale, showing salvation as a process rather than an event. He identified 22 typical stages in a person's journey from first becoming aware of the supernatural but with no knowledge of Christianity, to a mature faith functioning within the body of Christ.

By using the marriage paradigm, we accomplish essentially the same thing. Plus, we use language that anyone can understand—and we reduce 22 stages to five:

- **INTRODUCTION** – A relationship begins when the parties are introduced and are attracted to each other. The journey towards transformation and integration begins when people are introduced to Jesus.

- **COURTSHIP** – Next, these two parties enter a period of courtship. They learn about each other, and about their families. In the transformation process, people get to know more about Jesus and his family, and they consider if they want to invest in this relationship, so it will grow.

- **ENGAGEMENT** – The engagement period begins when both parties decide they want to commit their futures to each other. They state their intent to marry. Likewise, people decide they want to commit themselves to Jesus as their Lord and Savior.

- **THE WEDDING** – Finally comes the wedding, where the two parties publicly commit their lives to each other. Baptism is the equivalent in the transformation process—a public "marriage to Jesus," in the context of the church family.

- **MARRIED LIFE** – Now the couple begins living out their covenant relationship on a daily basis, growing in their love for each other. In the same way, new believers begin to live out their relationship with Jesus and his family, growing together towards maturity and fruitfulness in service to God's kingdom.

Now, to illustrate this paradigm, I'll use a concrete example—the process by which I entered into a lifelong relationship with my wife, Gwen. Like most analogies, this one isn't perfect. For example, 17 months passed from the time I first met Gwen until we were married. That doesn't imply it should take 17 months for a person to move from being introduced to Jesus until being baptized as a believer. Some people will require less time, and some more. But I do believe this paradigm will prove helpful in developing a healthy model for passing on the good news of God's kingdom.

Introduction

As a college sophomore in early 1968, I was in the middle of a down time. My grandmother, who had lived with our family all my life, passed away exactly five months before her 100th birthday. Her death was immediately followed by the end of the first semester, which I finished with the lowest grades of my life—and with little motivation to begin another term.

But the biggest blow was yet to come. I had been dating a girl for almost two years, but I knew it wasn't a healthy relationship. In the middle of a telephone call one evening, my thinking cleared. I jumped in my car, drove to her house, and ended the relationship. Although I knew it was right, it was an emotional downer.

My cousin and fellow college student, Helen, decided I needed a lift, and she had just the solution: I needed to meet Gwen, a friend and fellow nursing student. For two weeks I resisted her attempts to get us together. Then one evening, she invited my roommate and me to her apartment to play cards. As soon as I accepted, she went to get Gwen—who was about as excited about meeting me as I was about meeting her.

We spent the evening playing cards, and when it was time to go home, Helen "discovered" she had "lost her keys." I took Gwen home in my roommate's 1960 Cadillac—the one with the BIG fins. As I returned to my room, I realized I actually had enjoyed the evening. So, a week later I accepted an invitation to go bowling with Helen and several of her friends—including Gwen. As they say, the rest is history.

In a previous chapter, we said taking hold of the good news begins with hearing the truth. But often, if not always, there is a previous step: *someone prays.* Paul wrote to the Corinthians, "the god of this age has blinded the minds of unbelievers, so that they cannot see the light of the gospel of the glory of Christ, who is the image of God" (2 Cor. 4:4). It's like the minds of unbelievers are clouded, "so that they cannot see the light of the gospel." I doubt if this cloud ever lifts without someone interceding for the person.

In my case, as it relates to my relationship with Gwen, I'm sure my mother's prayers led to the opening of my eyes. The cloud of confusion and indecision lifted, and I was able to take action. I knew for a long time that my mother was praying for me, because she did not want to see me getting serious with a person who was not a Christian. She prayed rather than trying to talk me out of the relationship; she knew I was not in a frame of mind to listen.

The combination of Mother's prayers and the respectful persistence of my cousin resulted in my introduction to Gwen. As we got to know each other, we were drawn to each other. Likewise, the intercession and respectful persistence of a good friend are a powerful combination for introducing people to Jesus and the good news of the kingdom.

Would I have heeded the words of a stranger who thought I needed to meet someone? Probably not. Because I knew and trusted my cousin, it was easier to hear what she was saying. We find the same truth as we share the good news of the kingdom—people who know us and trust us will find it much easier to hear us. This means it's important to build solid relationships with people who don't yet follow Jesus.

As people are introduced to Jesus, the Holy Spirit begins drawing them to the Father (John 6:44). This opens the door for the next phase of the marriage paradigm.

Courtship

Because we felt drawn to each other, Gwen and I began to see each other more frequently. Over the course of the next year, we spent a lot of time together. We talked about our common faith in Christ. We shared our hopes and dreams for the future. We got to know each other's families. Our trust grew and our relationship deepened. We *understood* each other better. Soon it would be time to "pop the question."

In like manner, when people are introduced to Jesus and find they are drawn to the Father, they begin to spend more time with God. They read his Word and begin to discover his hopes and dreams for them. They get to know God's family better. Their trust of God deepens. They begin to *understand* the call of Jesus to "Come, follow me!" They are moving toward the next phase.

Engagement

The day finally came when I knew I wanted to spend the rest of my life with Gwen as my wife. I think she was beginning to wonder if I would ever get around to asking the question. I did. She said, "Yes." And so we were engaged. It was our clear intention to follow through with a wedding, when we would officially begin married life.

During our engagement, we met several times with the pastor who would marry us. We were getting ready to say to each other, "I take you to be my wife (or husband), from this day forward, for better for worse, for richer for poorer, in sickness and in health, to love and to cherish, and to be faithful to you alone, till death us do part." The pastor wanted to be sure we *understood* what we were doing. He wanted to know we were truly committed and ready for married life.

The equivalent of engagement in the process of entering into an intimate, eternal relationship with God comes when people encounter God and invite Jesus to take charge of their lives. It is a clear statement of intent, as they pray and invite Jesus in.

Is the person "saved" at this point? Would they go to heaven if they died? The answer—as unsatisfying as it may be—is that we don't know. The regeneration of the human spirit in a new spiritual birth is the Holy Spirit's work. God knows when this happens, but we don't. We can only give "assurance of salvation" at this point if our faith is in a formula. An evangelist friend realized this several years ago. He told me, "We used to say 'John got saved last night.' Now we say, 'John prayed to receive Jesus last night.' Now we will see if he has been saved."

Many people come to this point, pray the prayer of engagement—and then end up stuck in dysfunctional and sinful lifestyles, while totally convinced they are Christians. Let's stop "assuring" people of something we don't know for sure, for we risk confirming them in their sin. Why not rather celebrate their engagement, their statement of intention, and then help them prepare for a wedding and a lifetime of faithful and fulfilling married life. As fruit of transformation becomes evident, then we can say with confidence, "God has been at work here! There has been a new birth into God's kingdom."

The Wedding

I don't remember the date my wife and I were engaged. I do remember the day we were married. At 2 p.m. on Sunday afternoon, July 20, 1969, we were married in the Church of God in the small town of Idaville, Indiana.

Two hours later, we were trying to conduct a reception on the front lawn at Gwen's parents' house, while many of our guests crammed into the living room, watching the *second* most important event of the afternoon—Apollo 11 landing on the moon! We watched Neil Armstrong take his "one small step for a man, one giant leap for mankind" from our honeymoon hotel later that night. It seemed to take him forever to get off that ladder!

In this analogy, baptism is the equivalent of the wedding. Just as a wedding is the public celebration of two persons' commitment to each other, so baptism is the public celebration of a person's commitment to Jesus as Lord, Savior, and King. In the wedding, the bride and groom repeat marriage vows. In baptism, new believers, who are part of the bride of Christ, repeat their baptismal vows to Jesus, the bridegroom.

On their wedding day, the bride and groom officially become part of each other's family—a daughter-in-law or son-in-law. Likewise, in baptism the new believers celebrate their entrance into God's family. Only here they are not in-laws, but full daughters and sons.

Married Life

One sad fact of our day is that many young couples put excessive time, energy and money into a wedding, while investing very little effort into their married life. While a wedding *is* a celebration, the wedding day is really just the first day of married life. I don't remember much about our wedding except the Apollo 11 landing—and our ring bearer picking up all the flowers that our flower girl dropped. But I have a wealth of memories from more than 40 wonderful years of life together since our wedding day. And frankly, we share a common expectation that our best years are yet ahead.

In the same manner, baptism is a significant event and a time to celebrate. But the real significance is the everyday experience of living life in the context of a loving relationship with God in service to his kingdom. Let's not put all the emphasis on the beginning and forget the life-long journey. That's one reason there are so many divorces in our time—and one reason why so many pray a prayer but never live it out to discover the joy of living an integrated life.

A DAY OF GOOD NEWS

There is a remarkable Old Testament story about a time when Ben-Hadad, king of Aram (Syria), had laid siege to the city of Samaria. The siege, which cut off the city's food supply, lasted so long that a great famine occurred. Some people even resorted to cannibalism.

Four men with leprosy sat at the city gate. They recognized that times were desperate and they really had nothing to lose. So they said to each other:

> Why stay here until we die? If we say, 'We'll go into the city'—the famine is there, and we will die. And if we stay here, we will die. So let's go over to the camp of the Arameans and surrender. If they spare us, we live; if they kill us, then we die. (2 Kings 7:3,4)

That evening they went to the Aramean camp. To their amazement, they found it completely deserted. God had sent the sound of a great army ahead of them, and the entire Aramean army ran for their lives.

These four starving lepers entered the first tent, finding all the supplies left behind when the army deserted the camp. They ate and drank their fill and began to carry out silver, gold, and clothes. They hid these things, then entered a second tent, again hiding the things left there.

At this point, they realized what was happening—they were gorging themselves and carrying off the bounty, while Samaria's inhabitants were still in the city, nearly starved to death. They said to each other, "We're not doing right. *This is a day of good news* and we are keeping it to ourselves" (7:9, emphasis added).

They returned to the city and reported what they found. The king sent some men to confirm their report. At that point, the people went out and plundered the Aramean camp, and the city was again well fed and safe.

This is also *a day of good news*. As Paul wrote, "*Now* is the time of God's favor, *now* is the day of salvation" (2 Cor. 6:2, emphasis added). Some of us have been keeping this to ourselves, afraid of being rejected if we tried to share it with others.

May we all overcome our fears and follow the example of the four lepers of Samaria. May we be open and available as the Holy Spirit sends us into the midst of a fragmented and broken world. May we take them the ministry and message of reconciliation—the good news of the kingdom and the Lord Jesus. And above all, may we live it and share it effectively, so others may find the integrated life and experience *shalom!*

APPLICATION TO LIFE

1. What does it mean to you personally that God is a "Sent and sending God?" In what ways have you been sent?
2. What difference do you believe it would make if we followed the marriage paradigm in sharing the good news of Jesus and God's kingdom, rather than the sales paradigm?
3. What is God saying to you *now* about being sent?

EPILOGUE

"Stand at the crossroads and look;
ask for the ancient paths,
ask where the good way is, and walk in it,
and you will find rest for your souls."

Jer. 6:16

If you have made your way through this book, you likely are either a follower of Jesus open to new thoughts, or a seeker open to learning more about the good news that Jesus brought to earth so long ago.

If you are in this latter group, I trust this book has brought you more understanding of what it means to take hold of the good news of God's kingdom and of the Lord Jesus Christ. I pray that, as you stand at a crossroads, you will consider the ancient path that Jesus walked—and you will follow him and find rest for your soul.

If you are in the former group, thank you for staying with me as I have challenged some ideas which may be very dear to you. Along with others, you also stand at a crossroads. We are in a very critical period in church history. It is a time to think—to muse—not just a·muse with the majority. It is a time to restore the biblical truths necessary to transform and integrate our lives and our broken world. I pray you also will choose the good way and will walk in it.

Lyle E. Schaller was the most well-known church consultant in America—and maybe in the world—for much of the 20th century. At a retirement celebration, he was asked what his biggest failures were. After first considering this an unbelievably rude interruption to the celebration, he quickly concluded this was a very wise question. He identified four, concluding with this one:

> My fourth, and most serious, failure is a product of a combination of (a) age, (b) thirty-five years invested in consultations with congregations, (c) personal bias as a denominationalist, (d) excessive optimism about the usefulness of old wineskins, and (e) a natural tendency to study the trees rather than to see the forest. To be more precise, I was focusing on the renewal of the old and failed to see that *a new reformation in American Christianity already was well underway.*[1]

Schaller went on to raise two questions:

> First, is it really true that a new reformation is well underway? The safe answer is to wait and see. By the year 2075, we will know for sure, one way or the other. Those who cannot wait that long may want to review a few of the signs of the new reformation…The signs are there for those who can read.[2]

I won't be around in 2075, so I can't wait! I also think the signs are there for anyone with an open mind, who is willing to open their eyes and look around. There is a deep level of dissatisfaction with the status quo. The fragmentation in the church and in our world cries out for change. And this brings us to Schaller's second question:

> The second question for the reader is the same as the one faced by this author: Do you want to devote your time and energy to patching up the old wineskins, or do you want to help shape this new reformation? God is great! God is good! God also gives you that choice![3]

I first read these words of Schaller more than 12 years ago. I decided to spend the rest of my days helping shape this new reformation, this new apostolic paradigm of church.

I believe this is where we must begin—with our understanding of the gospel itself. The good news of the kingdom, proclaimed by

Jesus and the early church, *is* the good news that transforms. It's an integrating gospel for the increasingly fragmented world in which we live. As we take hold of it, we can help shape the new apostolic paradigm of church God is establishing in our time.

What about you? Does this message resonate as truth in your spirit? If so, we would love to connect with you. Together, we can make a difference!

NOTES

Introduction

[1] Peter Cheltschizki, The Net of Faith, Bohemia, 1440, quoted in Edmund Hamer Broadbent, The Pilgrim Church (Grand Rapids: Gospel Folio Press, 1999), 146.

[2] Gallup, George Jr., Religion in America—50 Years: 1935-1985. The Gallup Report, May 1985, Report No. 236, 12.

[3] George Gallup, Jr. and Timothy Jones, *The Next American Spirituality: Finding God in the Twenty-first Century* (Colorado Springs: Cook Communications, 2000), 32f.

[4] "integrate." Webster's Third New International Dictionary, Unabridged. Merriam-Webster, 2002. http://unabridged.merriam-webster.com (5 Jun. 2009).

[5] Dallas Willard, *The Divine Conspiracy: Rediscovering our Hidden Life in God* (San Francisco: HarperSanFrancisco, 1997), 40.

[6] Gallup and Jones, 15.

Chapter 1: Fractured, Fragmented, and Frazzled!

[1] From the musical *Hair*, 1968, then recorded by The 5th Dimension in 1969. http://www.lyricsbox.com/5th-dimension-the-lyrics-age-of-aquarius-vv2dwrs.html (04/09/2007)

[2] Charles A. Reich, *The Greening of America* (New York: Random House, 1970), 4.

[3] http://www.disastercenter.com/crime/ (04/09/2007)

[4] http://www.divorcemag.com/statistics/statsUS.shtml (11/29/2006)

[5] http://www.bankruptcyaction.com/USBankStats1980-2005.gif (04/09/2007)

[6] http://www.usatoday.com/news/health/2006-12-20-stress_x.html (12/20/2006)

[7] http://pediatrics.about.com/od/childabuse/a/05_abuse_stats.htm (11/29/2006)

[8] Sophia Voravong, "Warning Signs There, But Little Was Done, Neighbors Say," *Lafayette Journal and Courier*, March 23, 2005, sec A:8.

[9] "Chronic Illness Cost to Soar Without Lifestyle Changes," *Psychiatry News,* December 7, 2007, Volume 42, Number 23, page 12 © 2007 American Psychiatric Association. http://pn.psychiatryonline.org/ cgi/content/full/42/23/12 (02/14/2009)

[10] http://www.boutell.com/newfaq/misc/sizeofweb.html , (9/27/2007)

[11] Walter Truit Anderson, *Reality isn't What It Used To Be* (San Francisco: HarperSanFrancisco, 1990), 33.

[12] John Dewey, *A Common Faith*, (New Haven: Yale University Press, 1934), 87.

[13] Ravi Zacharias, *The Real Face of Atheism* (Grand Rapids: Baker Books, 2004), 79.

[14] http://www.online-literature.com/forums/showthread.php?t=28601 (6/25/2008)

[15] Jean-François Lyotard, "Introduction to The Postmodern Condition: A Report on Knowledge." http://www.idehist.uu.se/distans/ilmh/pm/lyotard-introd.htm (6/25/2008).

[16] Willard B. Frick, *Humanistic Psychology: Interviews with Maslow, Murphy, and Rogers.* (Columbus, OH: Merrill Publishing Company, 1971), 107.

[17] Stanley Fish, *There's No Such Thing as Free Speech*, 1994, p.113, quoted by Crystal Downing, *How Postmodernism Serves My Faith*, 102.

[18] Ludwig Feuerbach, *The Essence of Christianity*, trans. by George Eliot (New York: Harper & Brothers, 1957), 270f.

Chapter 2: Fragmented Gospels, Fractured Lives

[1] A.W. Tozer, *The Best of A.W. Tozer*, ed. Warren W. Wiersbe (Grand Rapids: Baker Book House, 1978), 103.

[2] http://www.usatoday.com/news/religion/2008-12-18-saved-heaven_N.htm (12/18/08)

[3] Luther's words in Roland H. Bainton, *Here I Stand: A Life of Martin Luther* (New York: Penguin Books, 1955), 49f.

[4] http://www.usatoday.com/news/religion/2008-12-18-saved-heaven_N.htm (12/18/08)

[5] Dallas Willard, *The Divine Conspiracy: Rediscovering our Hidden Life in God.* (San Francisco: HarperCollins, 1997). See Chapter Two, "Gospels of Sin Management," for a more complete account of this problem.

[6] Tozer, 103, 104.

[7] Harold Bloom, *The American Religion*, (New York: Simon & Schuster, 1992), 37.

[8] Bloom, 30.

[9] Robert W. Funk, Roy W. Hoover, and The Jesus Seminar, *The Five Gospels: The Search for the Authentic Words of Jesus.* (New York: Polebridge Press, 1993), back cover

[10] Mark D. Roberts, "Unmasking the Jesus Seminar," http://www.markdroberts.com/htmfiles/resources/unmaskingthejesus.htm

[11] Robert W. Funk, "The Coming Radical Reformation: Twenty-one Theses," http://westarinstitute.org/Periodicals/4R_Articles /funk_theses.html

[12] Quoted by Mark D. Roberts, "Unmasking the Jesus Seminar,"

[13] John S. Spong, "A Call for a New Reformation," http://www.geocities.com/Athens/5029/heresy5.html

[14] Anne Lamont, *Traveling Mercies* (New York: Pantheon, 1999), p. 41, quoted in George Gallup Jr. and Timothy Jones, *The Next American Spirituality: Finding God in the Twenty-First Century* (Colorado Springs: Cook Communications, 2000), 58.

[15] E. Stanley Jones, *The Way*. (Nashville: Abingdon-Cokesbury Press, 1946), 10.

[16] Alan Wolfe, *The Transformation of American Religion: How We Actually Live Our Faith* (New York: Free Press, 2003), 2f.

Chapter 3: The Big Story of the Kingdom

[1] The heart of this diagram comes from George Eldon Ladd, *The Gospel of the Kingdom* (Grand Rapids: Eerdmans, 1959). See pp. 24-51. I have expanded it to give further clarity.

[2] William A. Beckham, *The Second Reformation: Reshaping the Church for the 21st Century* (Houston: Touch Publications, 1995), 84.

[3] Dallas Willard, *The Divine Conspiracy*, 21.

[4] For a fuller discussion of this, see Harley Swiggam, *The Bethel Series, Old Testament* (Madison, Wisconsin: Adult Christian Education Foundation, 1981). See pages 3-17.

[5] M. Scott Peck, *People of the Lie: The Hope for Healing Human Evil* (New York: Simon and Schuster, 1983), 182f.

[6] Alternate reading from the footnote in the TNIV

[7] John S. Spong, "A Call for a New Reformation," online article available at http://www.dioceseofnewark.org/jsspong/reform.html, (11/05/2002).

[8] Leslie Stahl interview with Bishop Spong, aired on CBS' "60 Minutes" 5/21/2000, CBS Worldwide Inc.

[9] "just." *The American Heritage Dictionary*, Electronic Edition, Third edition, Version 3.6p, © 1994, SoftKey International, Inc.

[10] George Eldon Ladd, *A Theology of the New Testament* (Grand Rapids: Eerdmans, 1974), 632.

Chapter 4: The Gospel of the Kingdom

[1] Alan Wolfe, *The Transformation of American Religion : How We Actually Live Our Faith* (New York: Free Press, 2003), 3.

[2] *The Pilgrim Hymnal*, 1904

[3] Dietrich Bonhoeffer, *The Cost of Discipleship* (New York: Macmillan, 1963), 45-48.

[4] Ralph W. Neighbour, Jr., *Survival Kit for New Christians: A Practical Guide to Spiritual Growth* (Nashville, TN: Convention Press, 1979). See pages 62-85 for a thorough discussion of these three aspects of our salvation.

[5] Robert K. Brown and Mark R. Norton, Editors, *The One Year Book of Hymns* (Wheaton: Tyndale House), Electronic edition (Cedar Rapids: Laridian), March 17 devotional reading by William J. Petersen and Randy Petersen.

[6] George Gallup, Jr., "Six Spiritual Needs of Americans," in *1992 Yearbook of American and Canadian Churches* (Nashville: Abingdon Press).

Chapter 5: Taking Hold of the Good News

[1] "believe." *Collegiate Dictionary*. Merriam-Webster, 2005. http://unabridged.merriam-webster.com/MWOL-home.htm (18 Aug. 2005).

[2] This is a very close, if not completely accurate, quote of Professor Roten's illustration, given in Basic New Testament Greek class at the Associated Mennonite Biblical Seminary, Summer 1978. This dear saint has gone to be with the Lord, so I have no way to verify her exact words.

[3] "integrity." Webster's Third New International Dictionary, Unabridged. Merriam-Webster, 2002. http://unabridged.merriam-webster.com (29 Jan. 2009).

Chapter 6: Living from the Center

[1] Harold E. Bauman, *Presence & Power: Releasing the Holy Spirit in the Life of Your Church* (Scottdale, PA: Herald Press, 1989), 75.

Chapter 7: Following Jesus in Formation

[1] Dallas Willard, The Spirit of the Disciplines: Understanding How God Changes Lives (San Francisco: HarperCollins, 1988), ix, 20.

[2] "discipline." Webster's Third New International Dictionary, Unabridged. Merriam-Webster, 2002. http://unabridged.merriam-webster.com (9 Mar. 2009).

[3] Information on *The Redeemer's Key* can be found at http://www.opendoorcf.org/resources.html.

[4] "habit." The American Heritage Dictionary, Electronic Edition, Third edition, Version 3.6p, © 1994, SoftKey International, Inc.

[5] C.S. Lewis, *The Screwtape Letters* (New York: The Macmillan Company, 1951), 15.

[6] Thomas à Kempis, *The Imitation of Christ*, translated by William C. Creasy (Macon, GA: Mercer University Press, 1989), 23.

[7] Dietrich Bonhoeffer, *The Cost of Discipleship*, translated by R. H. Fuller, revised by Irmgard Booth, 2nd edition (New York: Macmillan, 1959), 45.

[8] Willard, 156.

[9] Willard, 152.

[10] I especially recommend chapters eight and nine.

[11] Willard, 158.

[12] In an excerpt from *Worship, the Missing Jewel of the Evangelical Church*, reprinted in *The Best of A .W. Tozer*, compiled by Warren Wiersbe (Grand Rapids: Baker Book House, 1978), 217.

[13] George Barna, "Survey Shows Faith Impacts Some Behaviors But Not Others," THE BARNA UPDATE, October 22,2002, http://www.barna.org/FlexPage.aspx?Page=BarnaUpdate&BarnaUpdateID=123, accessed 03-03-2005.

[14] Calvin Miller, *The Table of Inwardness* (Downers Grove, IL: Inter-Varsity Press, 1984), 83.

[15] Quoted in Willard, 165.

[16] See Willard, Chapter Nine, "Some Main Disciplines for the Spiritual Life."

[17] Henry Cloud and John Townsend, *How People Grow: What the Bible Reveals about Personal Growth* (Grand Rapids: Zondervan, 2001), 122.

Chapter 8: Following Jesus in Community

[1] Georges Florovsky, "Empire and Desert: Antinomies of Christian History," quoted in Shane Claiborne and Chris Haw, *Jesus for President: Politics for Ordinary Radicals* (Grand Rapids: Zondervan, 2008), 226.

[2] Nathaniel Branden, *The Six Pillars of Self-Esteem* (New York: Bantam, 1994), 123.

[3] Branden, 296, 297.

[4] Brian Hathaway, *Living with the Saints We Know,* quoted at http://www.christianity.co.nz/church4.htm (5/23/2009).

[5] John Emory, ed. *The Works of the Reverend John Wesley*, VIII:468, quoted in D. Michael Henderson, *John Wesley's Class Meeting: A Model for Making Disciples* (Nappanee, IN: Evangel Publishing House, 1997), 118f.

[6] Contact Tony Stoltzfus at www.coach22.com.

[7] John Stott, *One People: Clergy and Laity in God's Church*:, quoted at http://www.christianity.co.nz/church6.htm (5/19/2009).

[8] Ken Sande, *The Peacemaker: A Biblical Guide to Resolving Personal Conflict*, Third Edition (Grand Rapids: Baker Books, 2004)

[9] Quoted in Dick Tripp, "Exploring Christianity," http://www.christianity.co.nz/author.htm (05/29/2009).

Chapter 9: Following Jesus in Mission

[1] Quoted by Howard Culbertson, at http://home.snu.edu/~HCULBERT/slogans.htm (06/01/2009). For more original content like this, please see this website.

[2] Michael Frost and Alan Hirsch, *The Shaping of Things to Come: Innovation and Mission for the 21st century Church* (Peabody, MA: Hendrickson Publishers, 2003). The seminar was held Sept 29-30, 2005 at Arden Hills, MN and is available for purchase on audio and video at http://www.lutheranrenewal.org/michael_frost_order_form.PDF.

[3] C. Peter Wagner, *Churchquake!* (Ventura, CA: Regal Books, 1999), 37.

[4] Loren B. Mead, *The Once and Future Church: Reinventing the Congregation for a New Mission Frontier* (Washington, D.C.: The Alban Institute, 1991). See Chapter 2, pages 8-29.

[5] This is a quote, as best I remember it, from a time that Shenk and I shared the platform at a mission conference a number of years ago.

[6] Mead, 68.

[7] http://www.empoweringthechurch.com/ncd_survey.htm (07/04/2009)

[8] For example, see Sharon Drew Morgan, *Selling With Integrity* (New York: Berkley Books, 1999).

[9] James F. Engel, *What's Gone Wrong With the Harvest: A Communication Strategy for the Church and World Evangelization* (Grand Rapids: Zondervan, 1975)

Epilogue

[1] Lyle E. Schaller, *The New Reformation: Tomorrow Arrived Yesterday* (Nashville: Abingdon Press, 1995), 13.

[2] Schaller, 13.

[3] Schaller, 14.

BIBLIOGRAPHY

Anderson, Walter Truit. *Reality isn't What It Used To Be.* San Francisco: HarperSanFrancisco, 1990.

Bainton, Roland H. *Here I Stand: A Life of Martin Luther.* New York: Penquin Books, 1955.

Barna, George. "Survey Shows Faith Impacts Some Behavior But Not Others." *THE BARNA UPDATE.* Oct 22, 2002. Mar 3,2005. http://www.barna.org/FlexPage.aspx?Page=BarnaUpdate&BarnaUpdateID=123

Bauman, Harold E. *Presence & Power: Releasing the Holy Spirit in the Life of Your Church.* Scottdale, PA: Herald Press, 1989.

Beckham, William A. *The Second Reformation: Reshaping the Church for the 21st Century.* Houston: Touch Publications, 1995.

Bishop Spong. Prod. Shari Finkelstein. "60 Minutes," May 21, 2000. Videocassette. New York: CBS Worldwide Inc, 2000.

Bloom, Harold. *The American Religion.* New York: Simon & Schuster, 1992.

Bonhoeffer, Dietrich. *The Cost of Discipleship.* Trans. R. H. Fuller, rev. Irmgard Booth, Second Edition. New York: Macmillan, 1959.

Branden, Nathaniel. *The Six Pillars of Self-Esteem.* New York: Bantam, 1994.

Broadbent, Edmund Hamer. *The Pilgrim Church.* Grand Rapids: Gospel Folio Press, 1999.

Brown, Robert K., and Mark R. Norton, Editors. *The One Year Book of Hymns.*Wheaton: Tyndale House, 1995, Electronic edition,Cedar Rapids: Laridian.

Claiborne, Shane, and Chris Haw. *Jesus for President: Politics for Ordinary Radicals.* Grand Rapids: Zondervan, 2008.

Cloud, Henry, and John Townsend. *How People Grow: What the Bible Reveals about Personal Growth.* Grand Rapids: Zondervan, 2001

Dewey, John. *A Common Faith*. New Haven: Yale University Press, 1934.

Downing, Crystal. *How Postmodernism Serves My Faith*. Downers Grove, IL: IVP Academic, 2006.

Engle, James F. *What's Gone Wrong With the Harvest: A Communication Strategy for the Church and World Evangelization*. Grand Rapids: Zondervan, 1975.

Feuerbach, Ludwig. *The Essence of Christianity*. Trans. George Eliot. New York: Harper & Brothers, 1957.

Frick, Willard B. *Humanistic Psychology: Interviews with Maslow, Murphy, and Rogers*. Columbus, OH: Merrill Publishing Company, 1971.

Frost, Michael, and Alan Hirsch. *The Shaping of Things to Come: Innovation and Mission for the 21st century Church*. Peabody, MA: Hendrickson Publishers, 2003.

Funk, Robert W. "The Coming Radical Reformation: Twenty-one Theses." http://westarinstitute.org/Periodicals/4R_Articles /funk_theses.html

Funk, Robert W., Roy W. Hoover, and The Jesus Seminar. *The Five Gospels: The Search for the Authentic Words of Jesus*. New York: Polebridge Press, 1993.

Gallup, George Jr. *1992 Yearbook of American and Canadian Churches*. Nashville: Abingdon Press, 1992.

____________. *Religion in America—50 Years: 1935-1985. The Gallup Report*. May 1985. Report No. 236.

Gallup, George Jr. and Timothy Jones. *The Next American Spirituality: Finding God in the Twenty-First Century*. Colorado Springs: Cook Communications, 2000.

Gumbel, Nicky. *The Alpha Course Manual*. Colorado Springs: Cook Ministry Resources, 1995.

Henderson, D. Michael. *John Wesley's Class Meeting: A Model for Making Disciples*. Nappanee, IN: Evangel Publishing House, 1997.

Jones, E. Stanley. *The Way*. Nashville: Abingdon-Cokesbury Press, 1946.

Ladd, George Eldon. *A Theology of the New Testament*. Grand Rapids: Eerdmans, 1974.

____________. *The Gospel of the Kingdom*. Grand Rapids: Eerdmans, 1959.

Lewis, C.S. *The Screwtape Letters*. New York: The Macmillan Company, 1951.

Lamont, Anne. *Traveling Mercies*. New York: Pantheon, 1999.

Mead, Loren B. *The Once and Future Church: Reinventing the Congregation for a New Mission Frontier*. Washington, DC: Alban Institute Publications, 1991.

Miller, Calvin. *The Table of Inwardness*. Downers Grove, IL: Inter-Varsity Press, 1984.

Morgan, Sharon Drew. *Selling With Integrity*. New York: Berkley Books, 1999.

Neighbour, Ralph W. *Survival Kit for New Christians: A Practical Guide to Spiritual Growth*. Nashville: Convention Press, 1979.

Peck, M. Scott. *People of the Lie: The Hope for Healing Human Evil.* New York: Simon and Schuster, 1983.

Reich, Charles A. *The Greening of America*. New York: Random House, 1970.

Roberts, Mark D. "Unmasking the Jesus Seminar," http://www.markdroberts.com/htmfiles/resources/unmaskingthejesus.htm

Sande, Ken. *The Peacemaker: A Biblical Guide to Resolving Personal Conflict*, Third Edition. Grand Rapids: Baker Books, 2004.

Schaeffer, Francis A. *Francis A. Schaefer Trilogy: The Three Essential Books in One Volume.* Wheaton: Crossway Books, 1990.

Schaller, Lyle E. *The New Reformation: Tomorrow Arrived Yesterday.* Nashville: Abingdon Press, 1995.

Snyder, Howard A. *Liberating the Church: The Ecology of Church & Kingdom.* Downers Grove: InterVarsity Press, 1983.

Spong, John S. "A Call for a New Reformation." Nov 5, 2002. http://www.dioceseofnewark.org/jsspong/reform.htm

Stahl, Leslie. Interview with Bishop Spong, aired on CBS' "60 Minutes" 5/21/2000, CBS Worldwide Inc.

Stott, John R.W. *Christian Counter-Culture: The Message of the Sermon on the Mount.* Downers Grove: InterVarsity Press, 1978.

Swiggam, Harley. *The Bethel Series.* Madison: Adult Christian Education Foundation, 1981.

The American Heritage Dictionary, Electronic Edition, Third Edition, Ver. 3.6p, CD-ROM. SoftKey International, Inc. 1994.

Thomas à Kempis. *The Imitation of Christ*. Trans. William C. Creasy. Macon, GA: Mercer University Press, 1989.

Tozer, A.W. *The Best of A.W. Tozer.* Ed. Warren W. Wiersbe. Grand Rapids: Baker Book House, 1978.

Voravong, Sophia. "Warning Signs There, But Little Was Done." *Lafayette Journal and Courier*. Mar 23, 2005, sec A: 8.

Wagner, C. Peter. *Churchquake!* Ventura, CA: Regal Books, 1999.

Webster's Third New International Dictionary, Unabridged. Merriam-Webster. Jun 30, 2005. http://unabridged.merriam-webster.com

Willard, Dallas. *The Divine Conspiracy: Rediscovering our Hidden Life in God.* San Francisco: HarperSanFrancisco, 1997.

____________. *The Spirit of the Disciplines: Understanding How God Changes Lives*. San Francisco: HarperCollins, 1988.

Wolfe, Alan. *The Transformation of American Religion: How We Actually Live our Faith*. New York: Free Press, 2003.

Zacharias, Ravi. *The Real Face of Atheism*. Grand Rapids: Baker Books, 2004.

ABOUT US

The Author

Dale Stoll served as Senior Pastor at Tri Lakes Community Church in Bristol, IN for 22 years, from 1979 to 2001. Dale and Gwen have been married since 1969 and have six children and six grandchildren. They are also foster and adoptive parents, and have had twenty-two foster children since 1990, three of whom they have adopted.

Dale is the founder and director of Radical Restoration Ministries, LLC. He is a graduate of Vincennes University, Purdue University, and attended the Associated Mennonite Biblical Seminary for three years.

Radical Restoration Ministries, LLC

Radical Restoration Ministries, LLC is called to partner with other likeminded leaders, congregations, networks, and movements to pioneer a new paradigm of church, assisting them in planting new churches and transitioning existing ones to this new paradigm. These new paradigm churches will be:

- Faithful to Biblical principles
- Focused on making mature disciples of Jesus
- Fruitful in 21st century western, postmodern culture—and in other cultures around the world where God opens doors

To this end, we provide the following ministries to the church:

- One, two, or three-day workshops on the subject of this book—*Integrated Lives*

- Coaching & Consulting ministries to assist you in navigating the difficult waters of transition to a new paradigm of church
- Networking ministries to connect you to other leaders, churches, and networks that long to see the integrating gospel of the kingdom lived out in our day

Restoration Press

Restoration Press publishes books and audiovisual resources for the church that provide a solid foundation upon which to see God's kingdom flourish. We also publish stories of the kingdom that will encourage others in their pursuit of following Jesus in everyday life.

Contact us:

We would love to hear from you and network with you!

- dale@radicalrestoration.org
- www.radicalrestoration.org
- www.restorationpress.com